STRANGE GUTS
AMERICAN SEPTIC
by Brian J. Orlowski

Copyright © 2011 Brian J. Orlowski All Rights Reserved.
ISBN: 0-9845801-9-0
ISBN-13: 978-0-9845801-9-4
Library of Congress Control Number: 2011937651

All rights reserved. No part of this book may be reproduced or transmitted in any form or by any means, electronic or mechanical, including photocopying, recording, or by any information storage and retrieval system, without permission in writing from the publisher or author.

This book is a work of fiction. People, places, events, and situations are the product of the author's imagination. Any resemblance to actual persons, living or dead, or historical events is purely coincidental.

First Published by *AuthorMike Dark Ink*, 10/15/2011

www.AuthorMikeInk.com

AuthorMike Ink, *Dark Ink* and its logo are trademarked by *AuthorMike Ink*.

Printed in the United States of America

This book is completely and utterly dedicated to my mother, Madeline. Without her support and belief in me, I'd have given up on being published decades ago. She is my angel, my sounding board, my therapist, my confidante, and most importantly, my best friend. Her faith in me has never waivered. How she put up with my behavior, insanity and antics for so many years is beyond me. I love you, mom.

A special thanks goes to Mark "Sparky" Dobrowolski, whose wit and wisdom helped shape, if not warp, Strange Guts in its infancy.

When I was in college oh-so-many years ago, I always wanted to do a comic strip. At the time, The Far Side was one of the most popular single-panel cartoons going. So I, in my wealth of experience and wisdom, decided to do my own version. A horror-based, full-out gory and funny single-panel comic strip. Oh, the accolades I would be showered in! How could it not be received well? Who wouldn't want to read it? Who wouldn't publish it? Well, pretty much *everyone*. I still have the folder filled with rejection letters, most of them impersonal form letters, some very personal, saying how horrible and unpublishable the content was.

15 years later, for fun, I dusted off my cartoons and posted a batch of them online. Surprisingly, to me at least, I found a new audience. That's the beauty of the Web — no matter how small a niche your demographic might be — you can reach your kind of people.

So when I was approached to publish my collection I was more than ecstatic. Not that I thought the comic would make me wealthy or famous. It was more that I was vindicated. Yes, somebody out there wanted to see Strange Guts published. Someone likes this most horrible, offensive, and gory comic strip. And most importantly, people want to read the book. I sleep better now and no longer run my car with the garage door closed.

The first half of the book contains gags from the early years of '94-'97. In the middle are a few I banged out in '05-'07, when I was getting back into cartooning after a long hiatus. The latter half of the book is replete with new gags, hopefully as good, maybe better, than the originals.

I hope you enjoy this book half as much as I enjoyed working on these cartoons for nearly 20 years.

Thanks very much,
Brian J. Orlowski

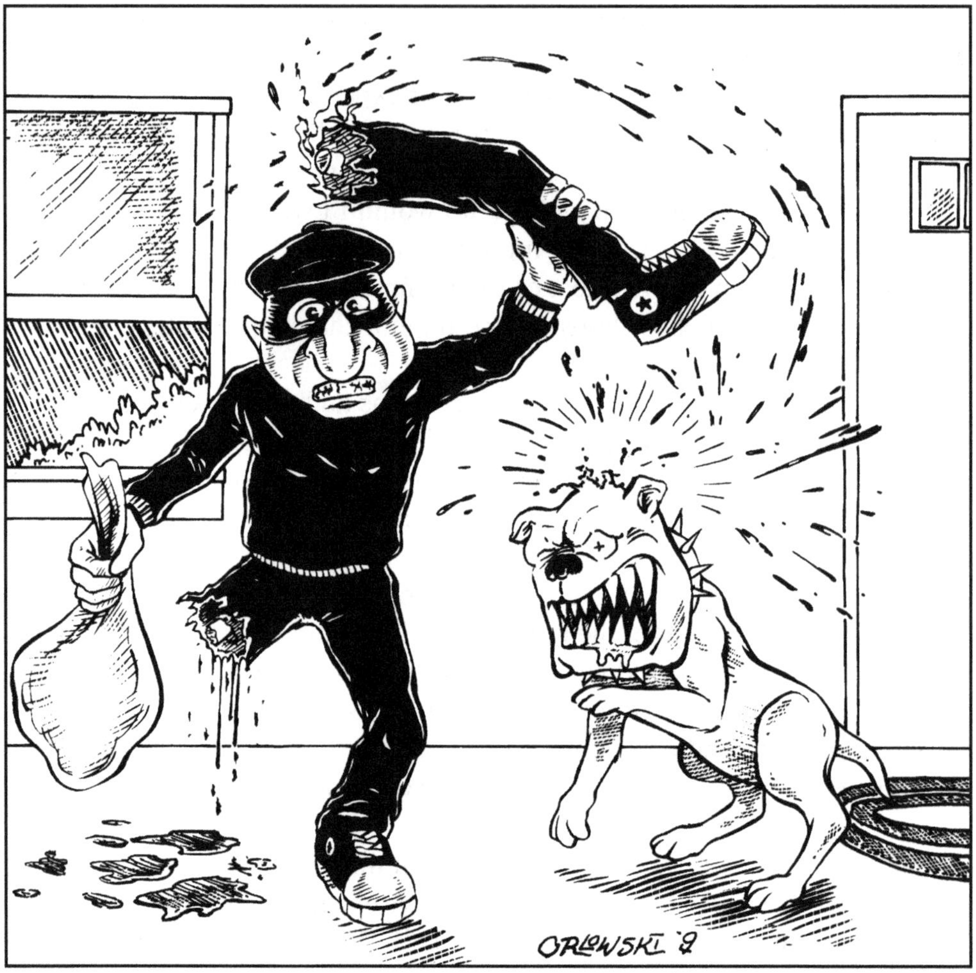
ORLOWSKI '8

Thinking quickly, Bob the thief ripped off his leg and beat the attack dog to death, thereby saving himself from harm.

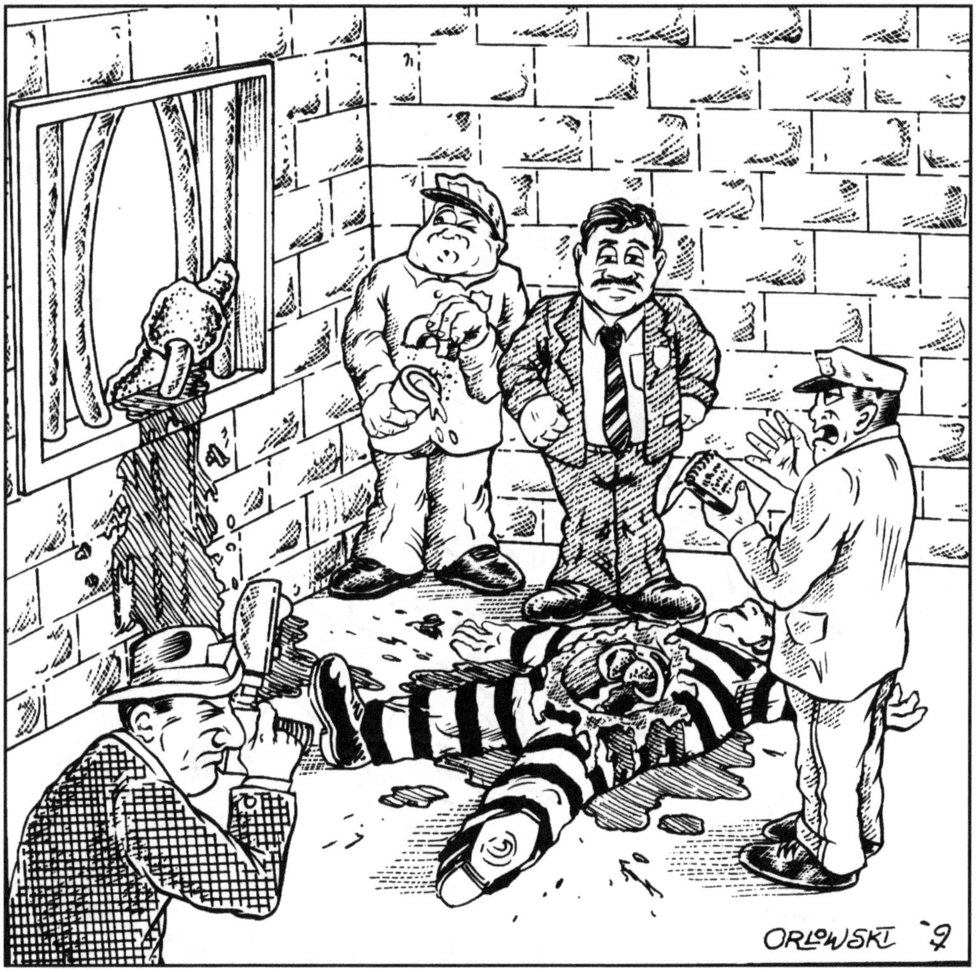
ORLOWSKI '9

"Seems to me, Chief, that
Jones ripped out his cellmate's
small intestine and used it to
climb down and escape."

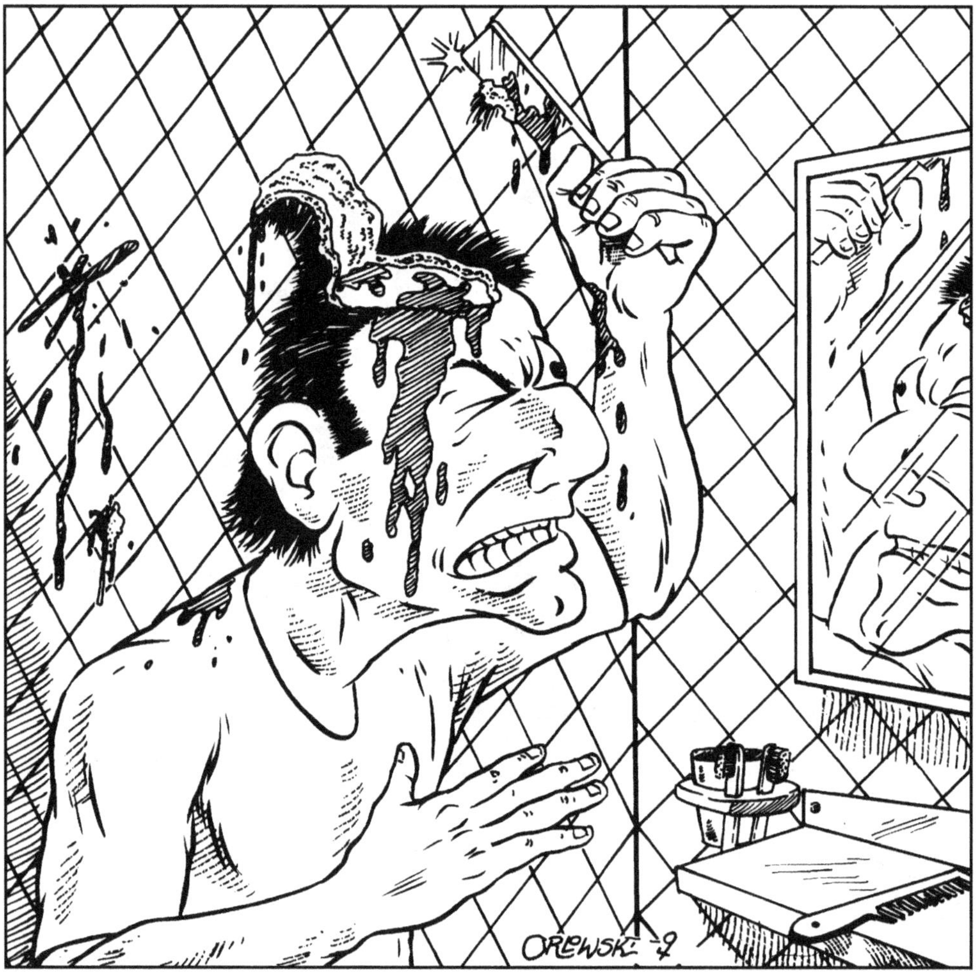
ORLEWSKI

Joey rushed to comb his hair,
and without thinking grabbed his razor by
accident, thereby creating the ultimate,
permanent reverse-mohawk.

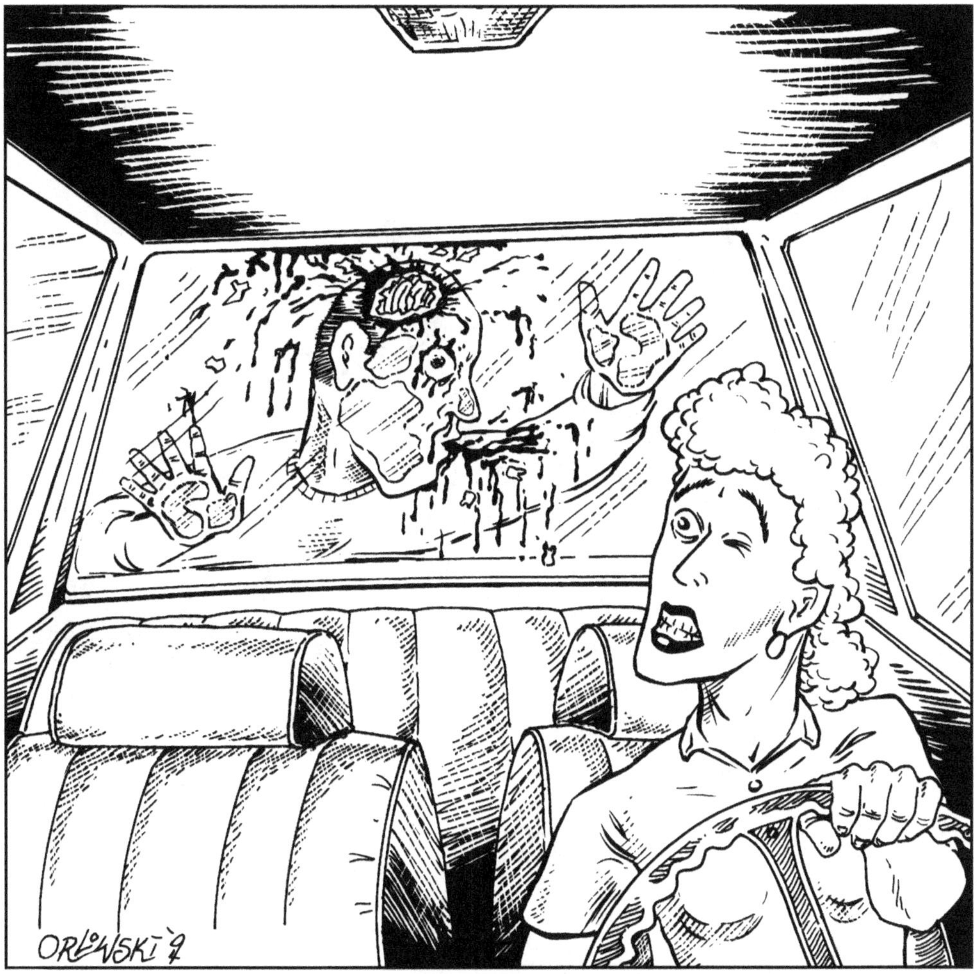
ORLOWSKI

Having backed the car violently
into her husband, Lori learned two things she
never knew: that shatterproof glass is for real
and her husband really did have a brain.

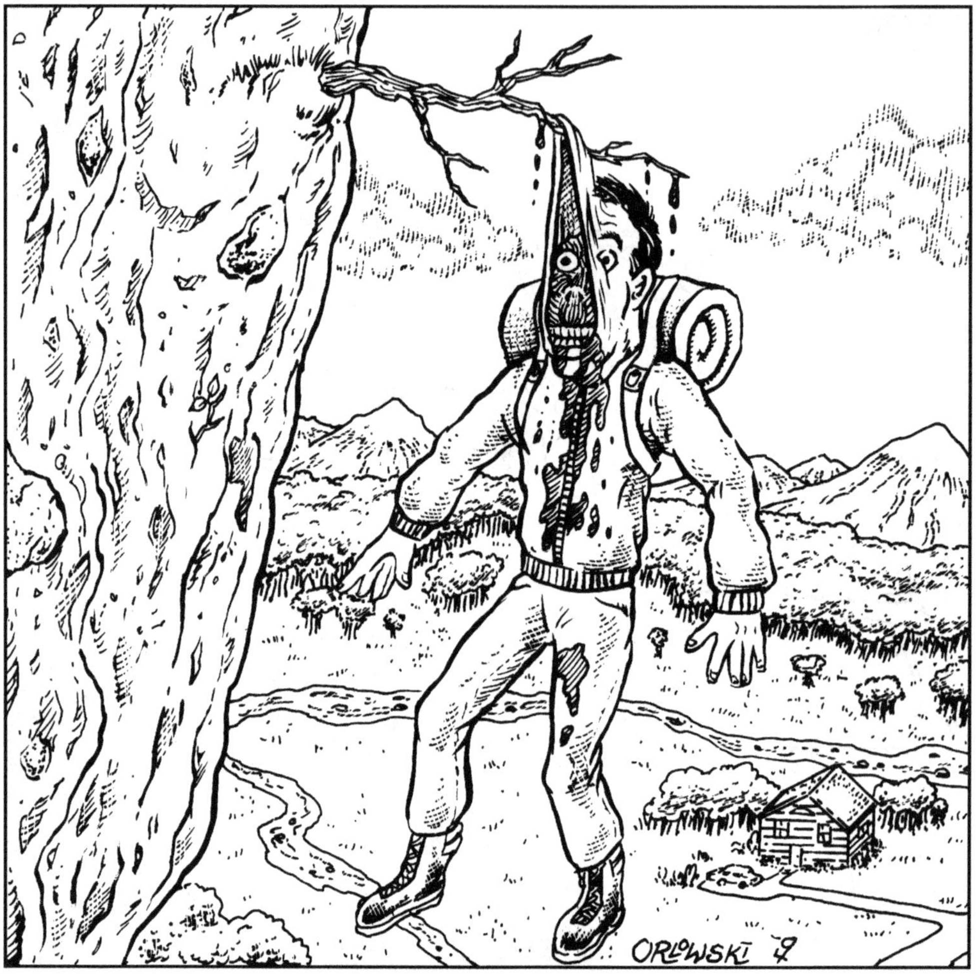
ORLOWSKI

By good fortune, Mortimer,
who was generally an unlucky fellow,
snagged a branch with his upper lip
when he fell off the cliff.

Considering it was their first date, Carla was worried that she had made a bad impression upon vomiting up a hand and pancreas, especially since they weren't her own.

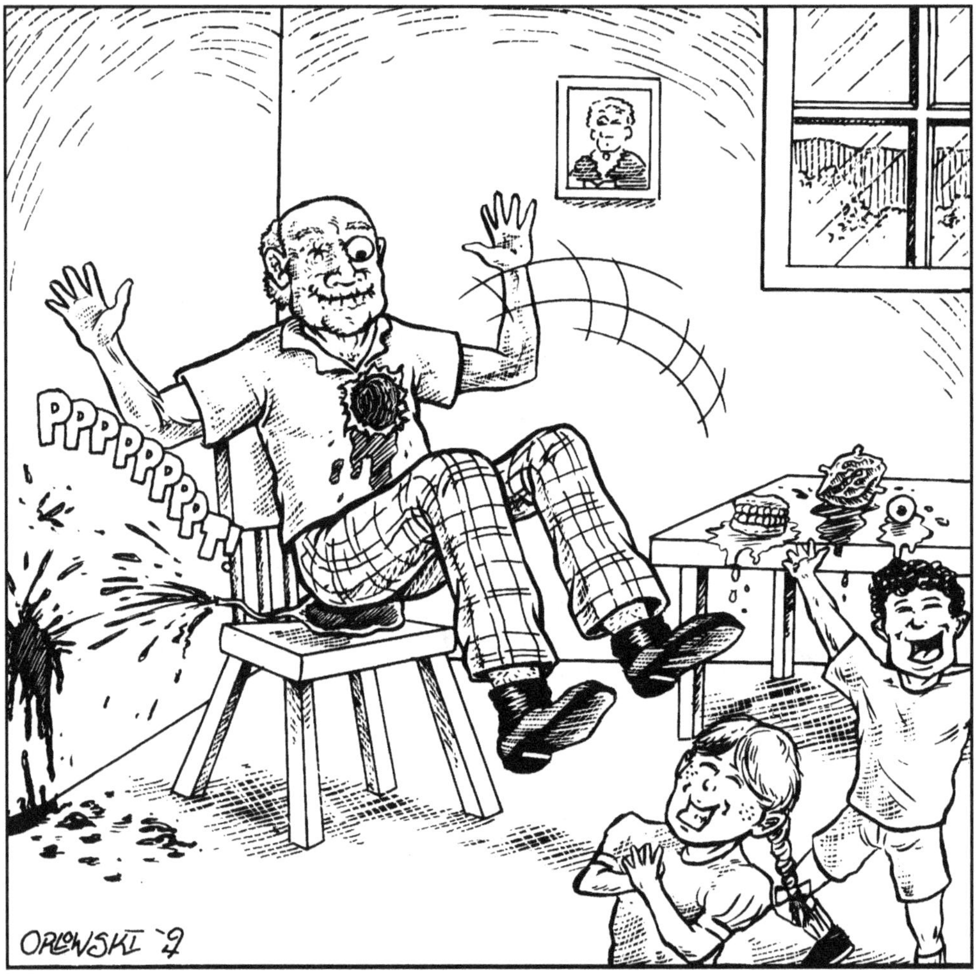
PPPPPPPPPPT!
ORLOWSKI '9

To entertain his grandchildren,
Ned would take out his false teeth,
glass eye, baboon heart, and use his
colostomy bag as a whoopie cushion.

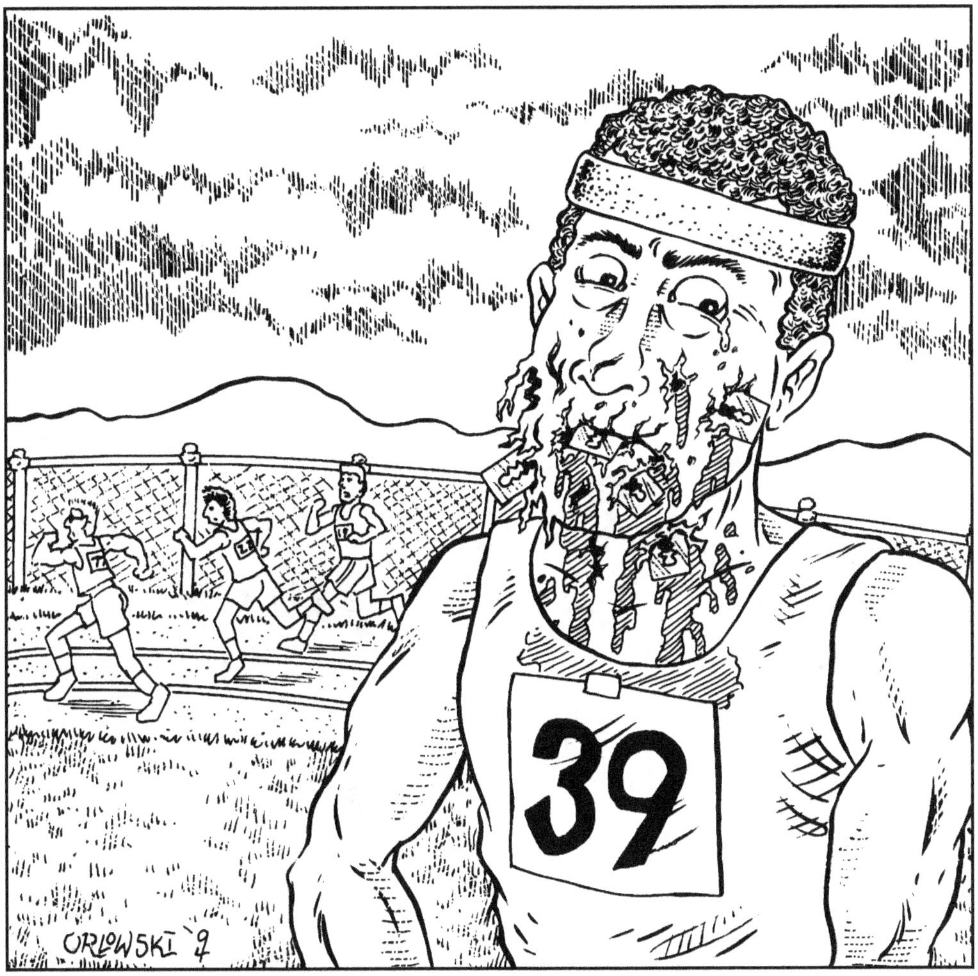
39
ORLOWSKI

It wasn't until after the embarrassing fall Gavin took in the fifth heat that the Olympic Committee decided to remove the *100-yard Dash with a Mouthful of Razorblades* event.

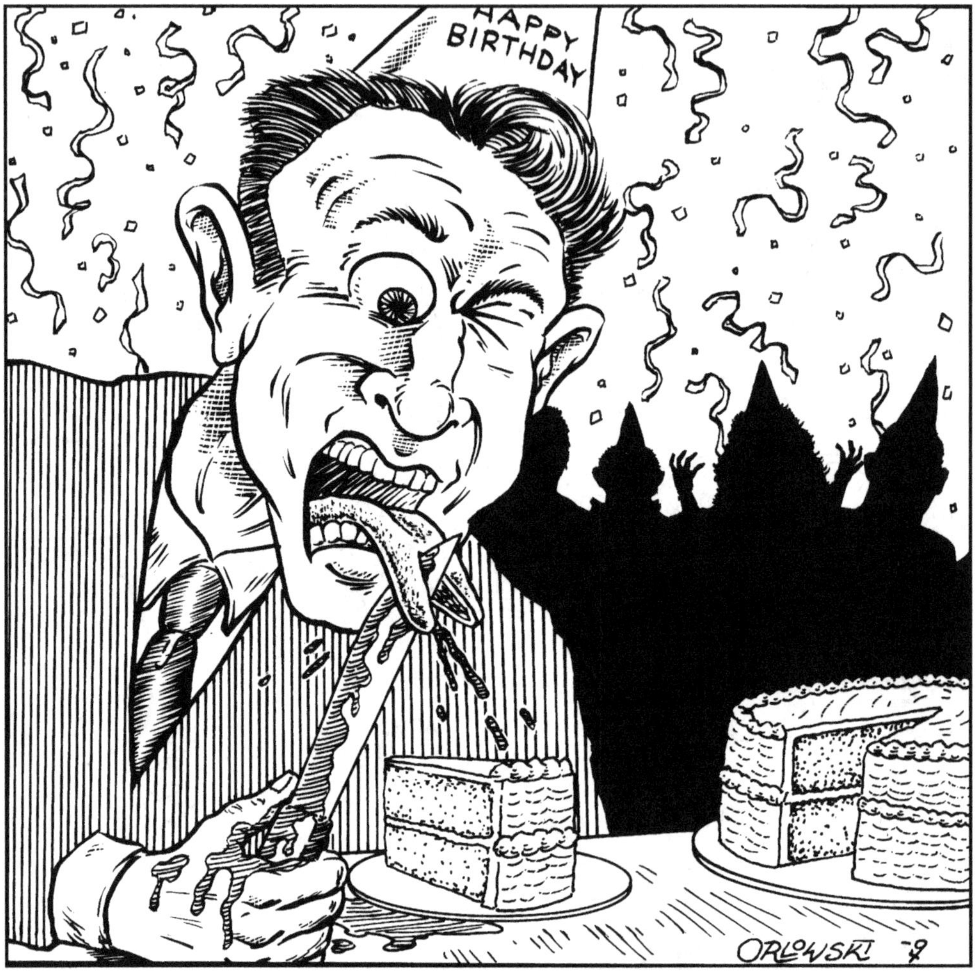
HAPPY
BIRTHDAY
ORLOWSKI '09

On his 35th birthday,
Wayne painfully learned not
to lick the icing off of
the cake knife.

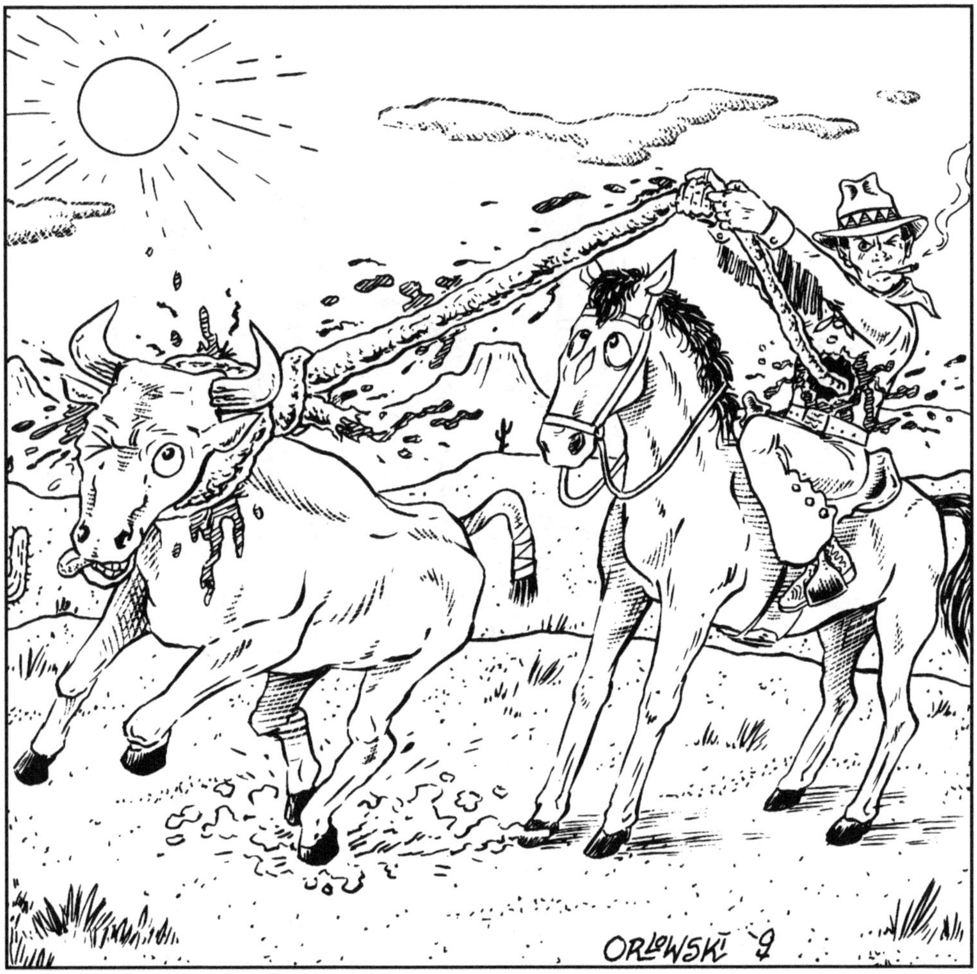
ORLOWSKI

Seeing the steer leading the cattle
toward a cliff, Luke, having no rope handy,
quickly used his small intestine to lasso the
bull and save the cattle drive, forever earning
the nickname, "Colon Hand Luke".

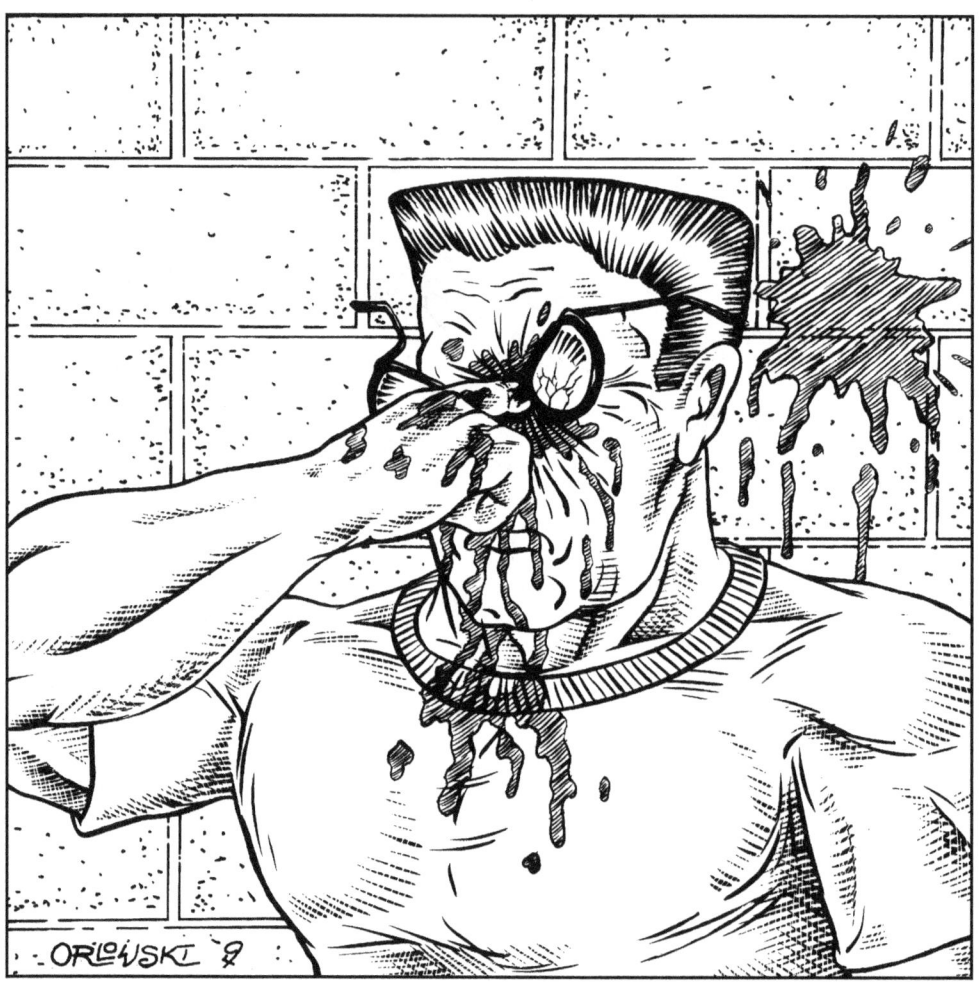

It was very unfortunate that George, who only moments ago gained super-human strength, wore glasses that always slid down his nose.

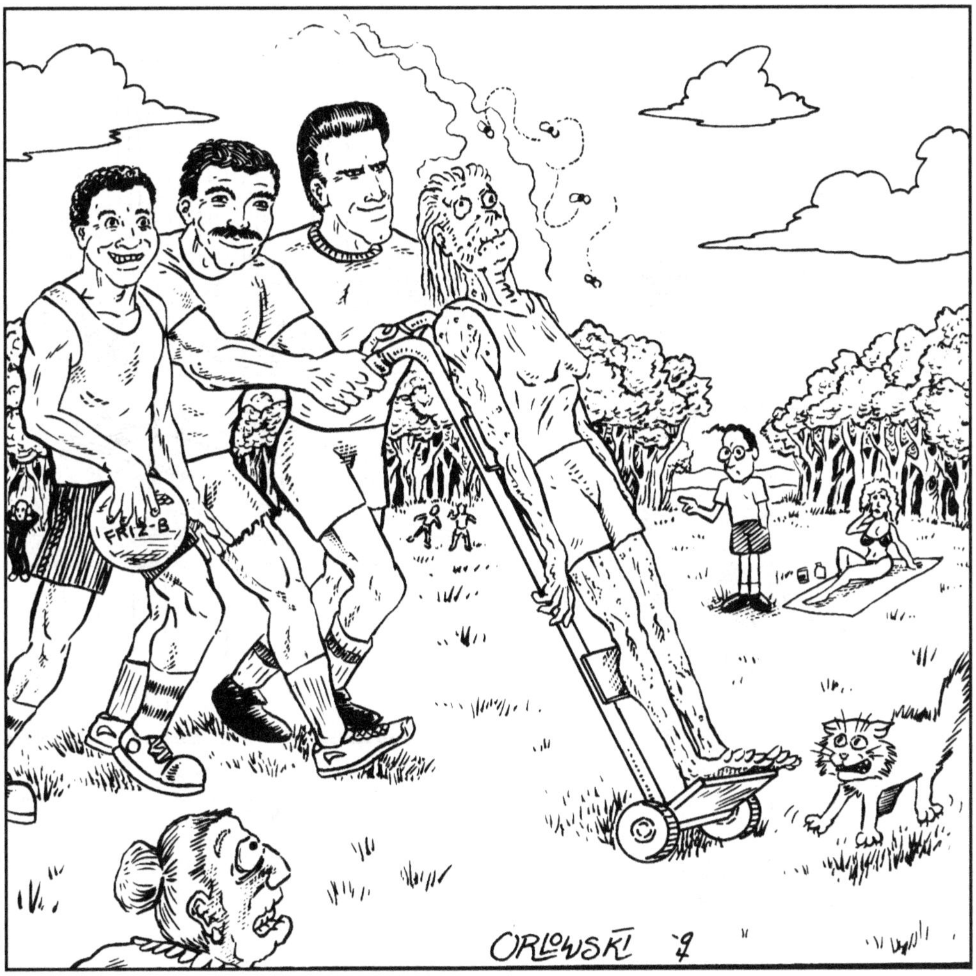
FRIZ-B
ORLOWSKI '9

Not well received by
either audiences or critics, was the
release of the final film in the series,
"Three Men and a Corpse".

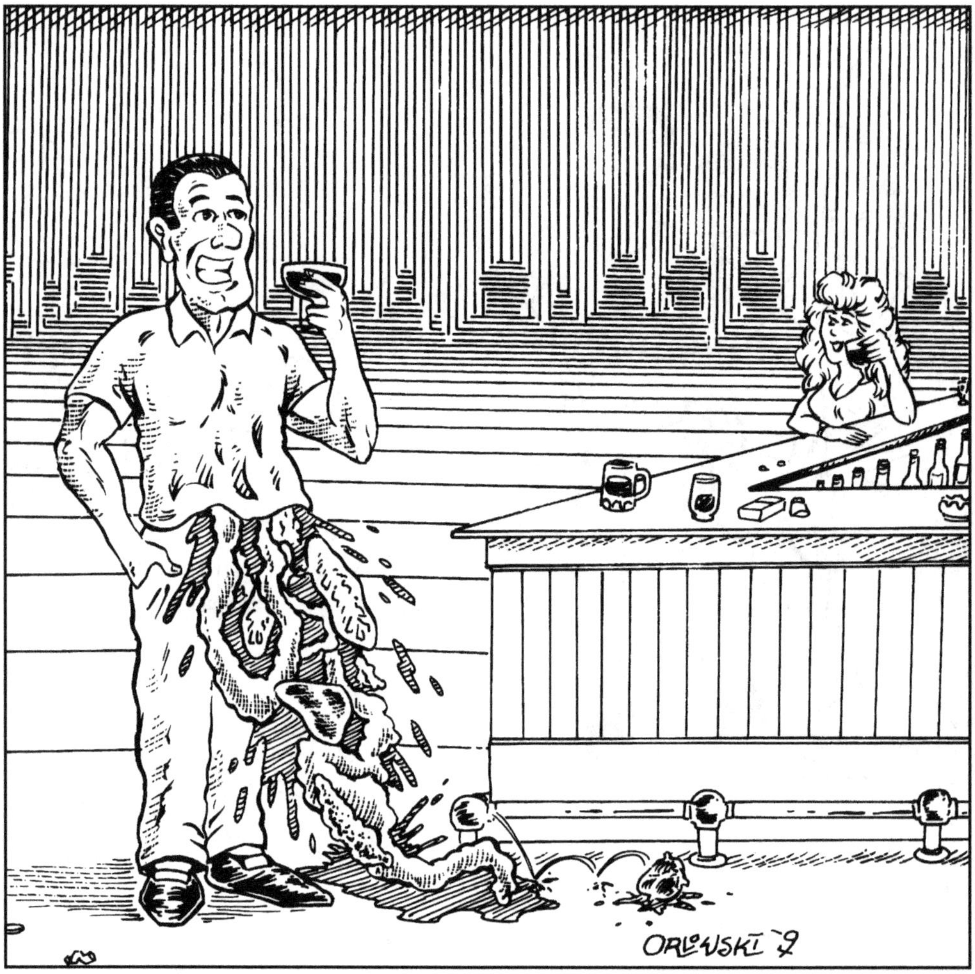
ORLOWSKI '9

Their eyes met from across the room, then as bad luck would have it, all of Sid's innards spilled to the ground, as they had sporadically done for years.

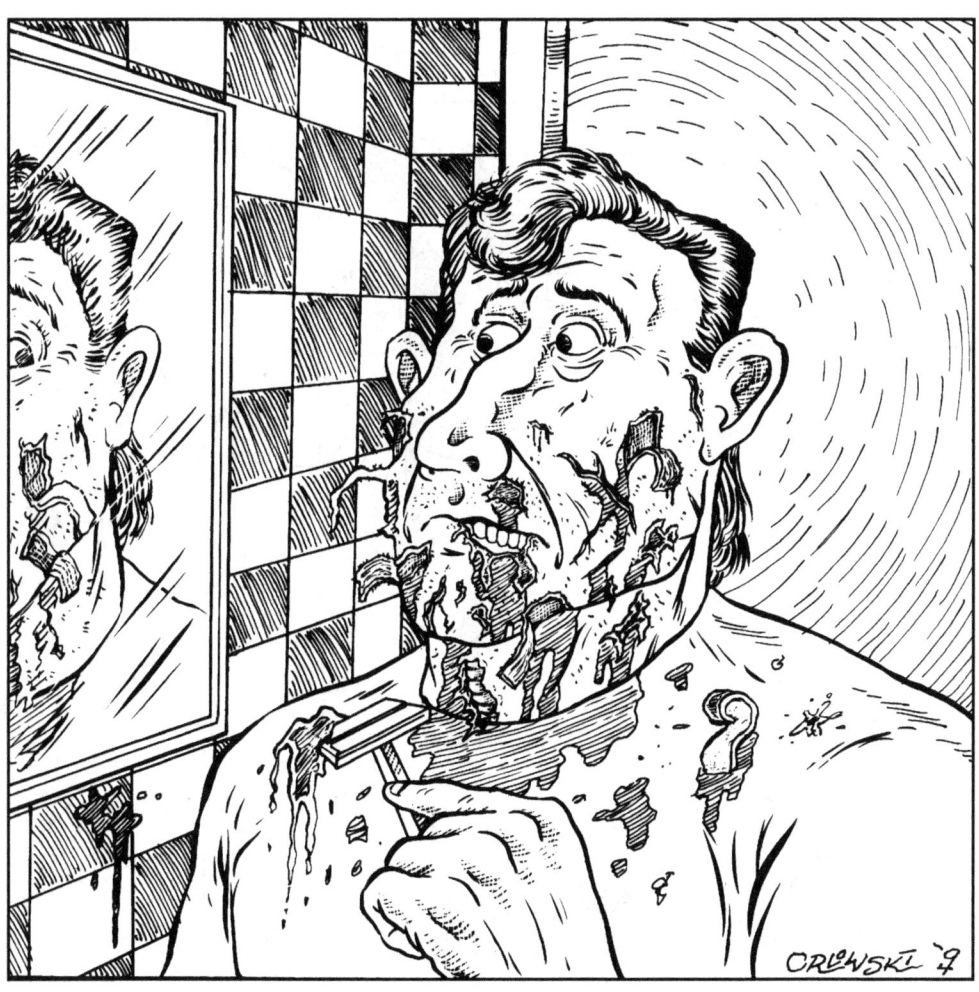

After much procrastination, Jack finally admits to himself that seven years is too long a time to go between changing razor blades.

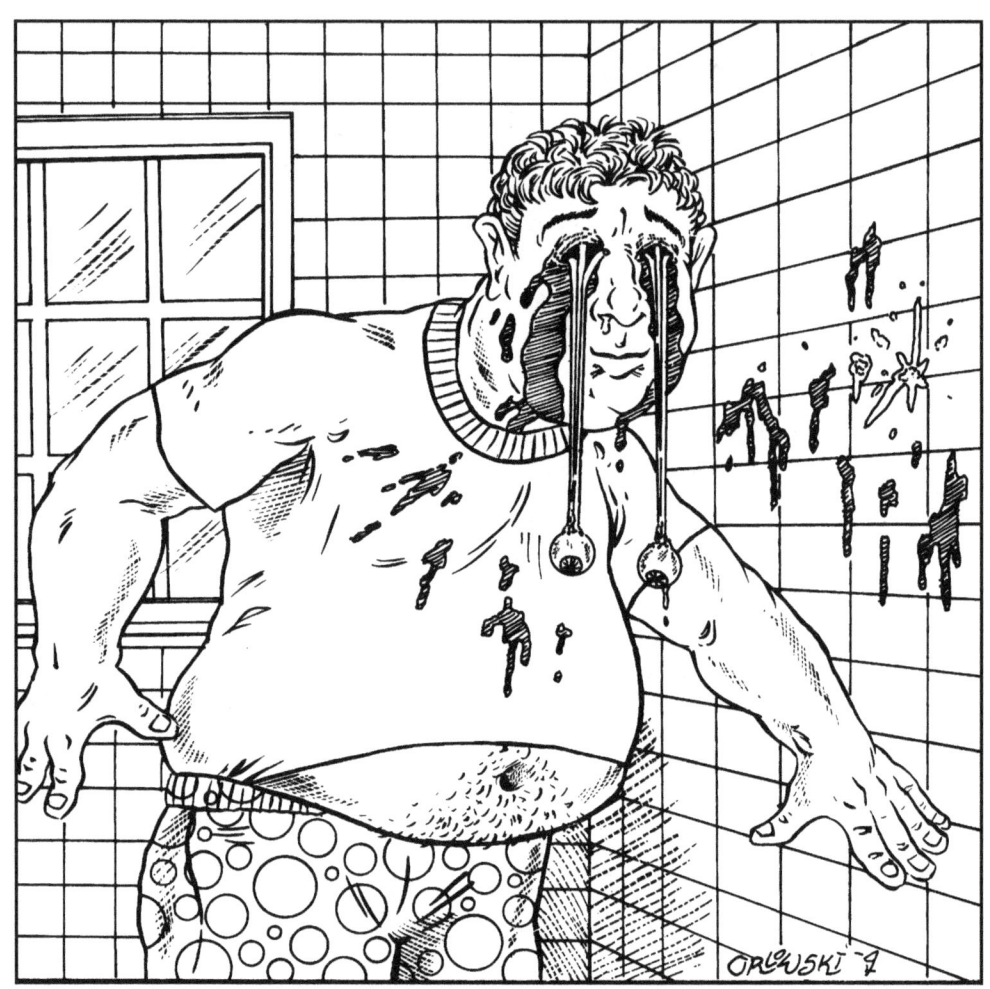

Fat Scott learned the hard way to never sneeze with your eyes open, but was more than thrilled to see his feet for the first time in years.

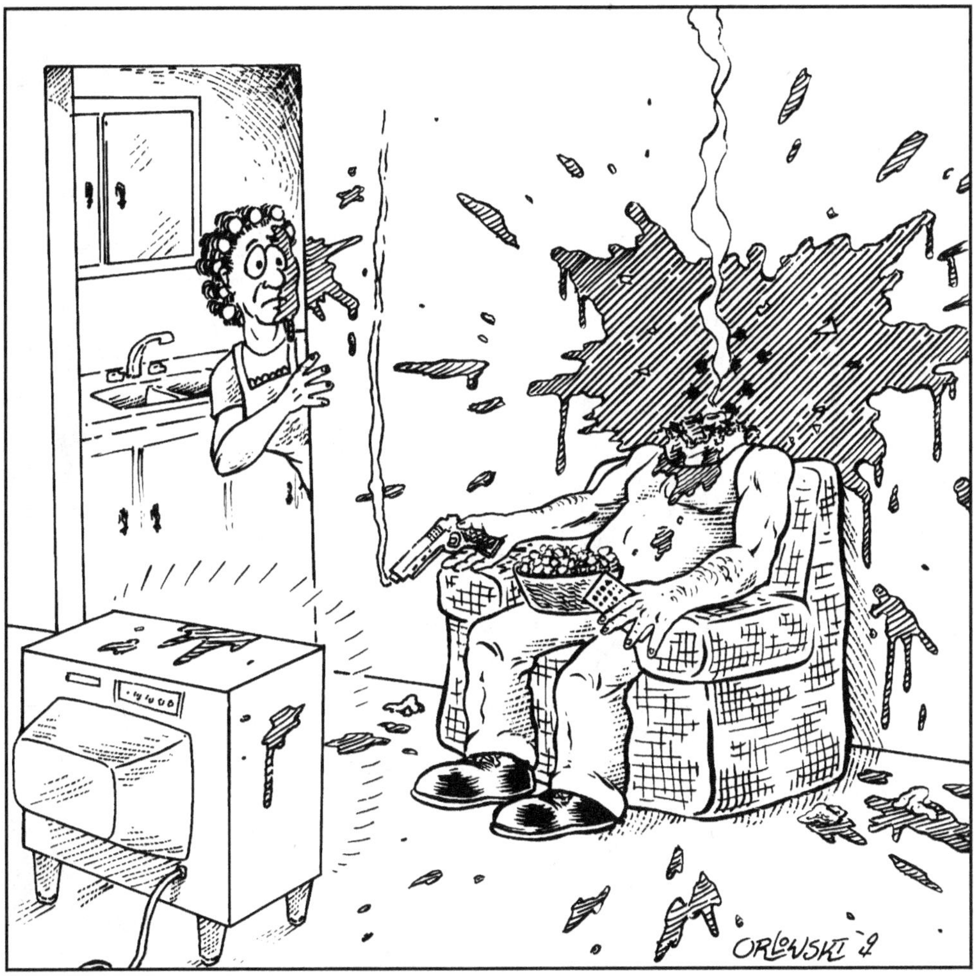
ORLOWSKI

"We now return to another episode in our 24-hour 'Brady Bunch' marathon where Cindy learns to overcome her lisp."

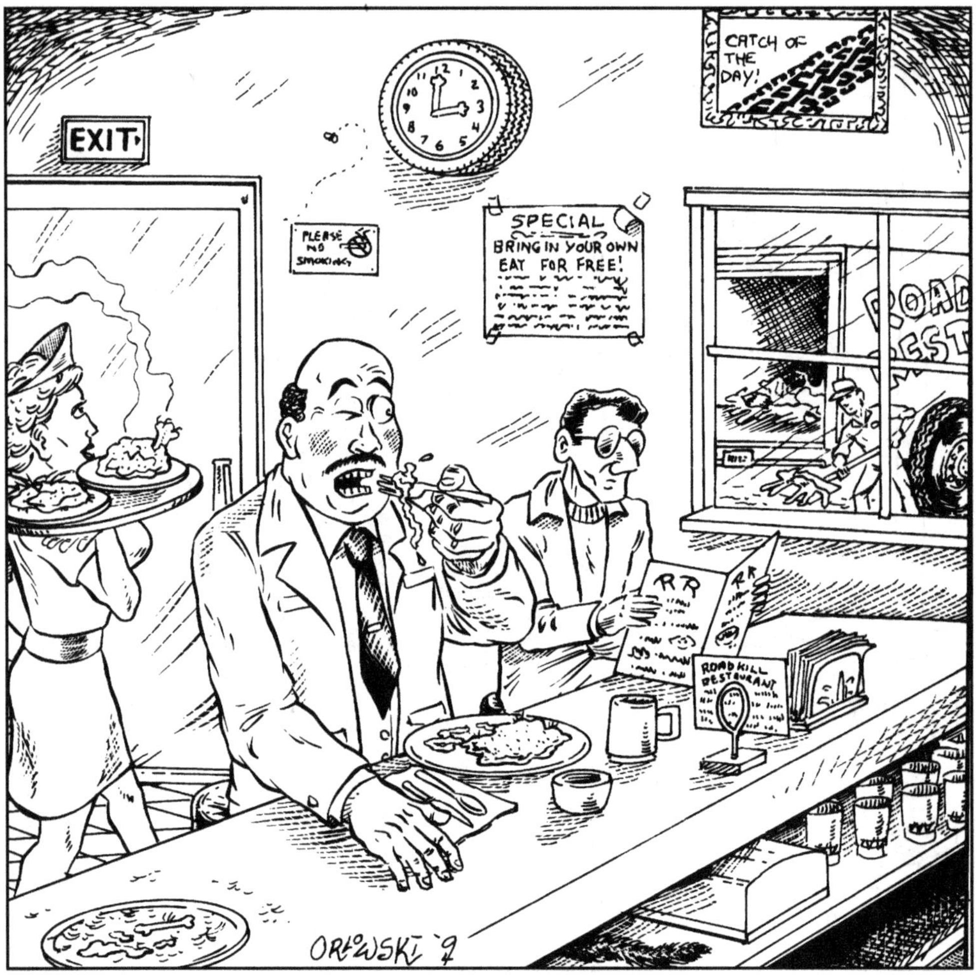
EXIT
CATCH OF THE DAY!
PLEASE NO SMOKING
SPECIAL
BRING IN YOUR OWN EAT FOR FREE!
RR
ROAD KILL RESTAURANT
ORLOWSKI '9

More than halfway through
his dinner, it dawned upon Ralph
exactly what was being served at
the Roadkill Restaurant.

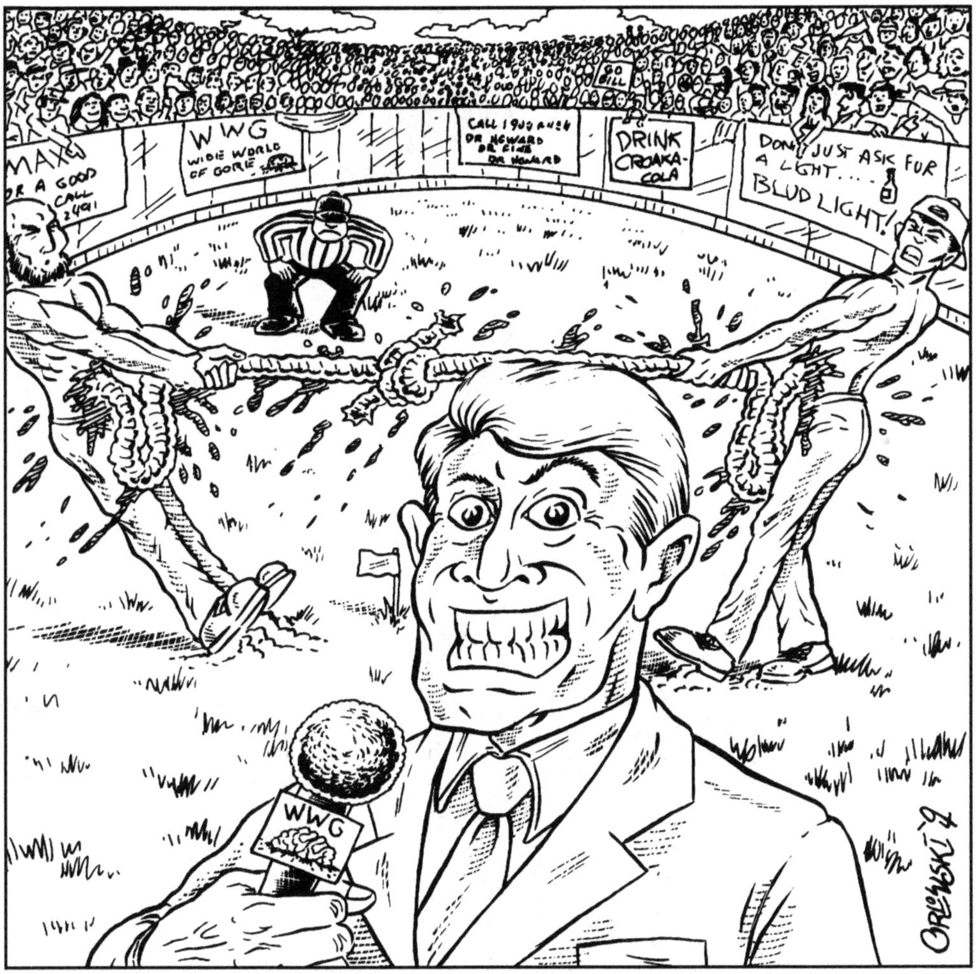
GO BILL
WWG
WIDE WORLD OF GORE
DR HOWARD DR FINE DR HOWARD
DRINK CROAKA-COLA
A LIGHT....
BLUD LIGHT!
WWG

"Hello everyone. This is Perry Toneum, reporting live from the 10th annual Last Will Games, opening today with its traditional intestinal pull event."

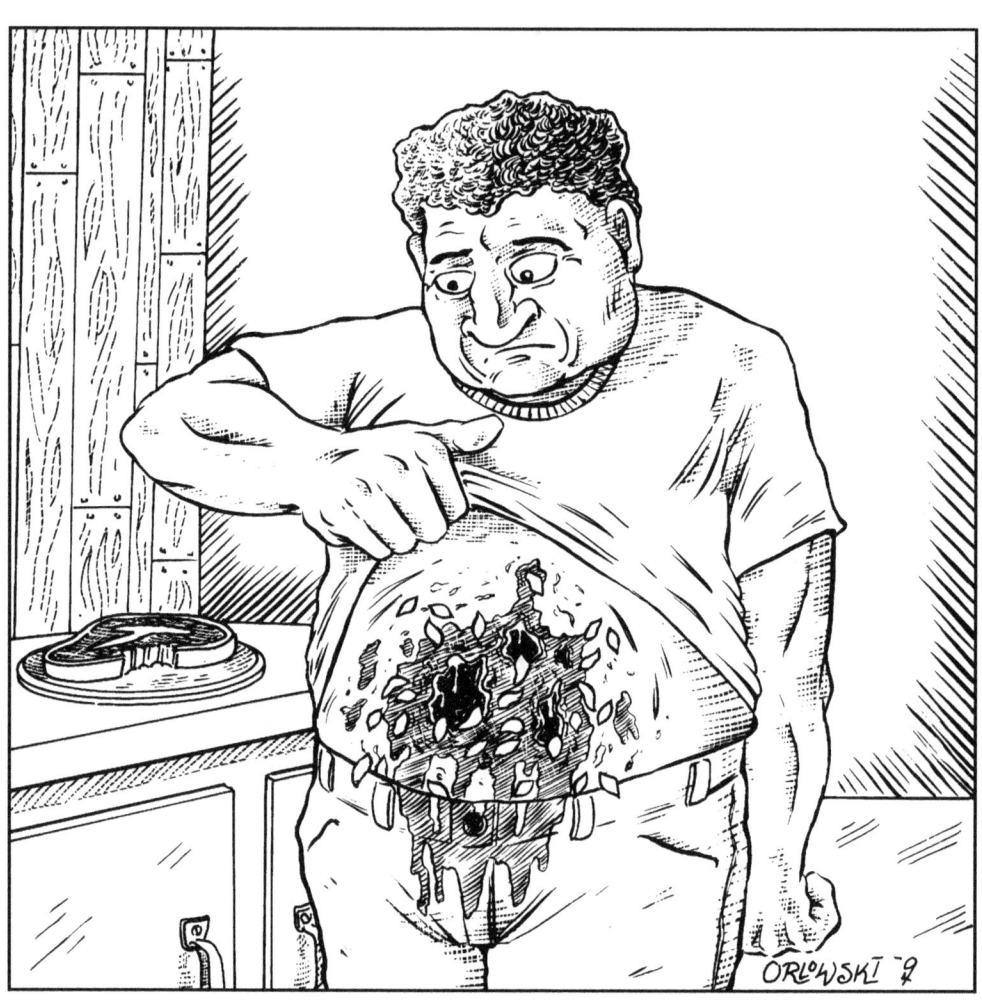

It wasn't until he noticed the maggots eating their way out of his stomach that Frank decided to stop dining on raw, unrefridgerated steak.

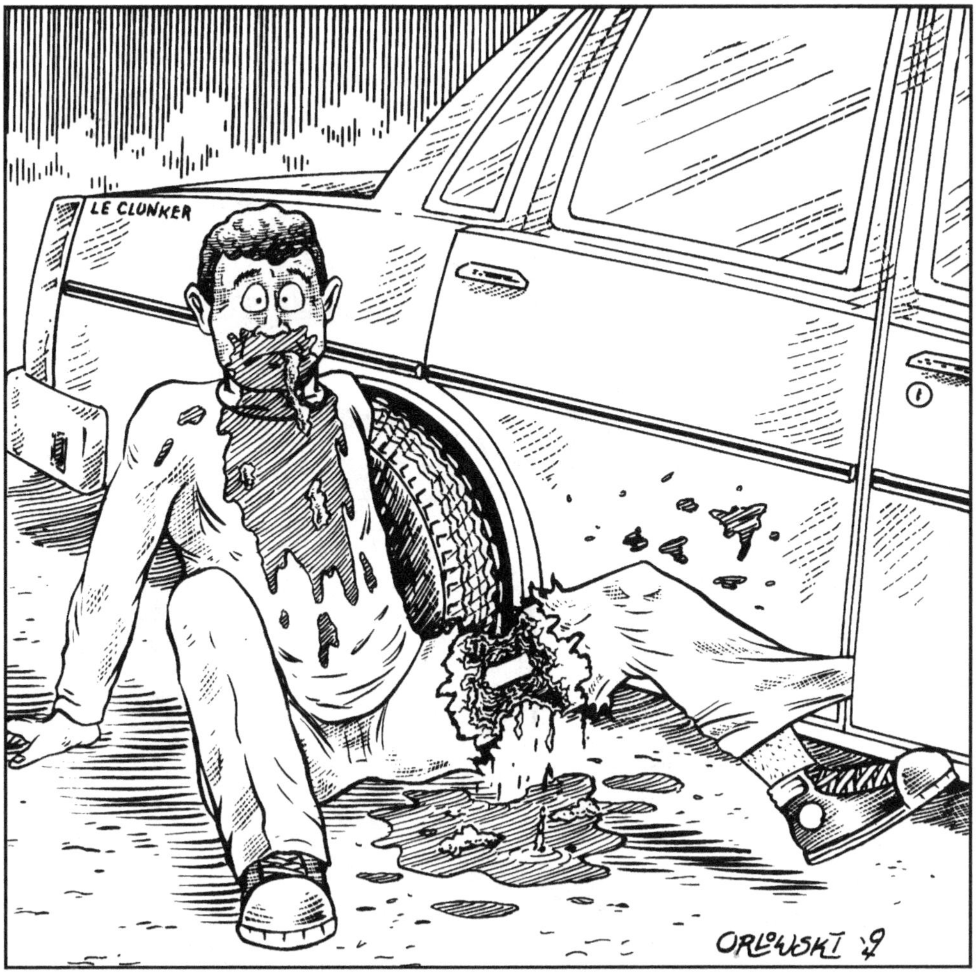
LE CLUNKER
ORLOWSKI '09

Accidently trapping his pantleg in
the car door, Norton, who had already chewed
halfway through his leg, realized he could have
simply taken his pants off.

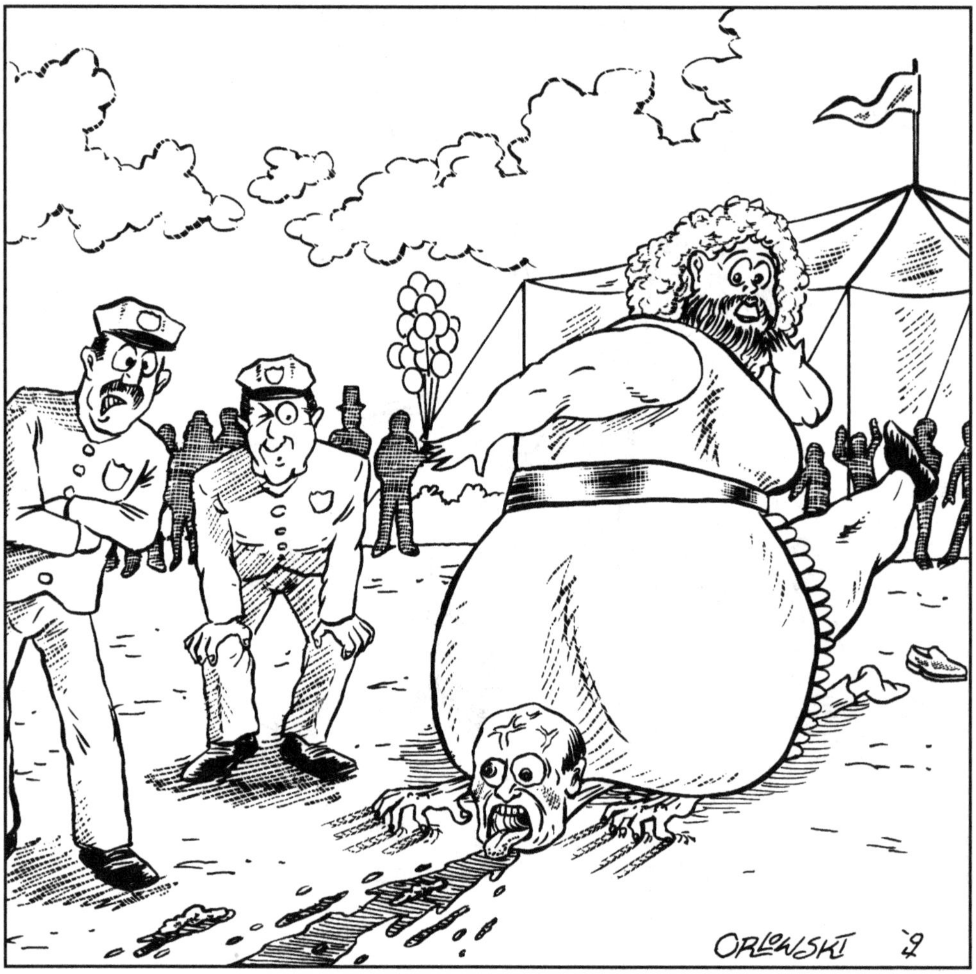
ORLOWSKI '9

After the investigation at the circus, the police decided to drop the first degree murder charge on the bearded fat lady, and filed the case under "Freak Accident".

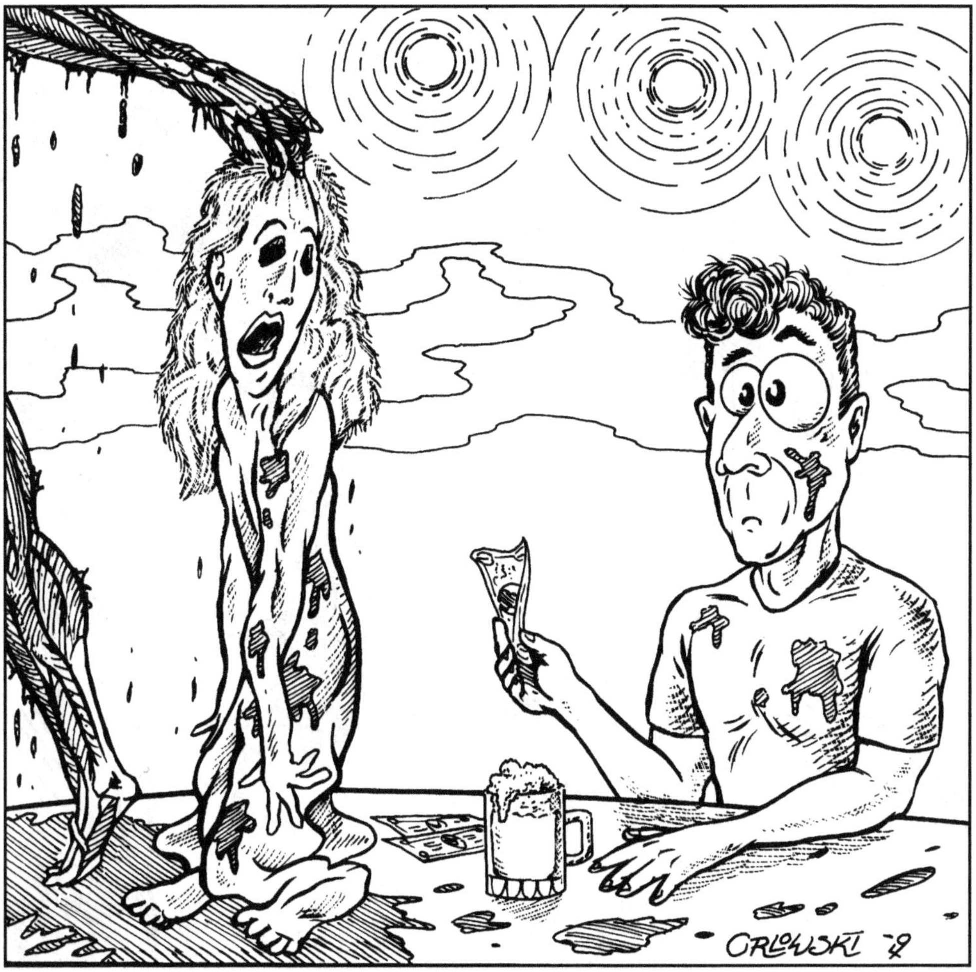
ORLOWSKI '08

Sparky thought he had seen everything at a strip club, but decided the dancer had gone too far when she ripped her skin off for a dollar.

After a few drinks too many,
Tim decided to clean his gun, and when his
wife later explained it to the police, she said
she had no idea that he was loaded.

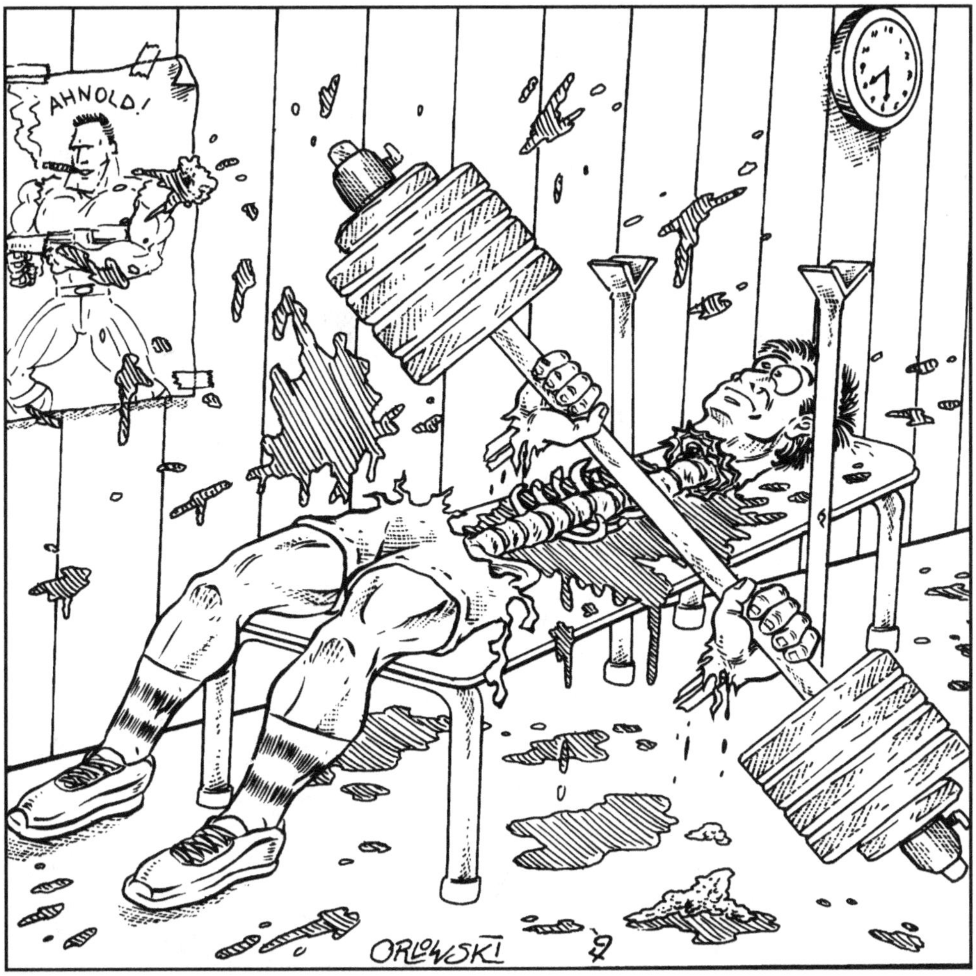
AHNOLD!
ORLOWSKI

Some say it was the steroids,
others say he'd pushed himself too hard, but
for whatever reason, on the night of October 13th,
Art's entire upper torso exploded.

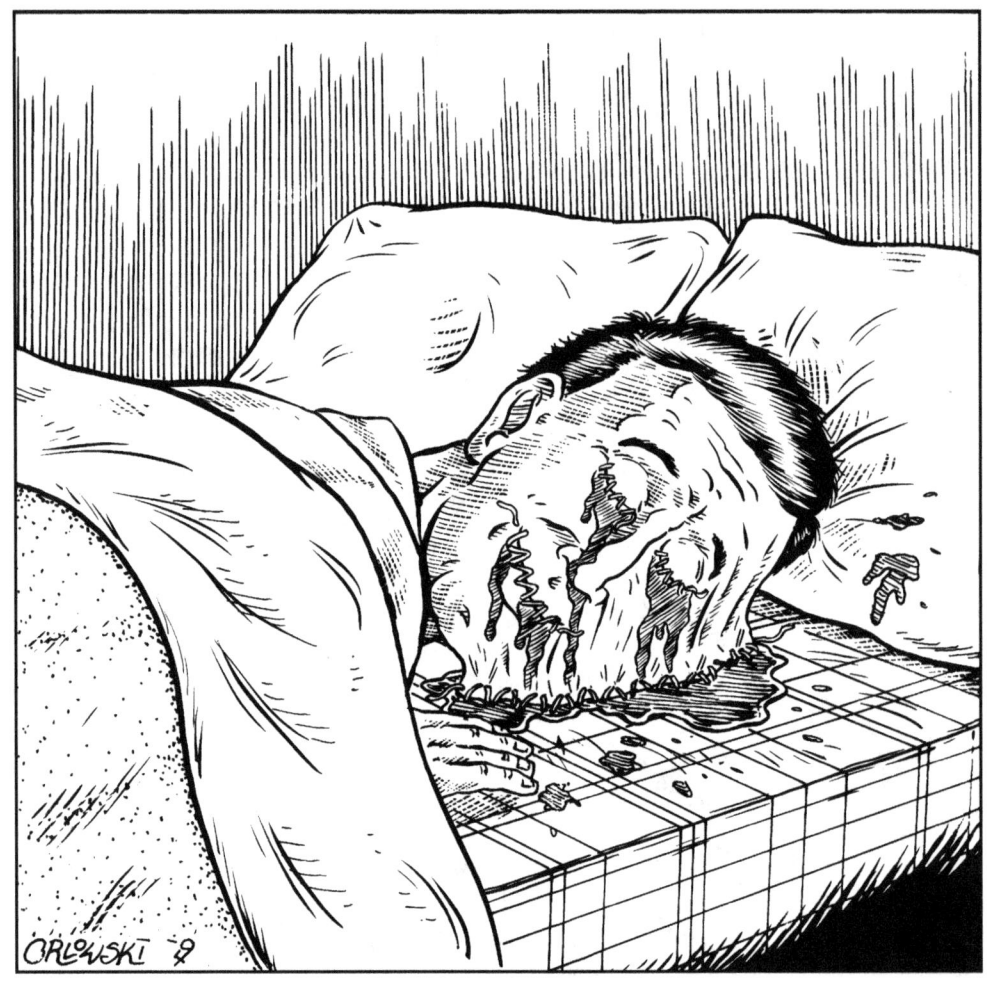

When Morris awoke to find his
eyes and lips sewn shut and his face sewn
to the sheets, he realized his wife got him
with another of her zany pranks.

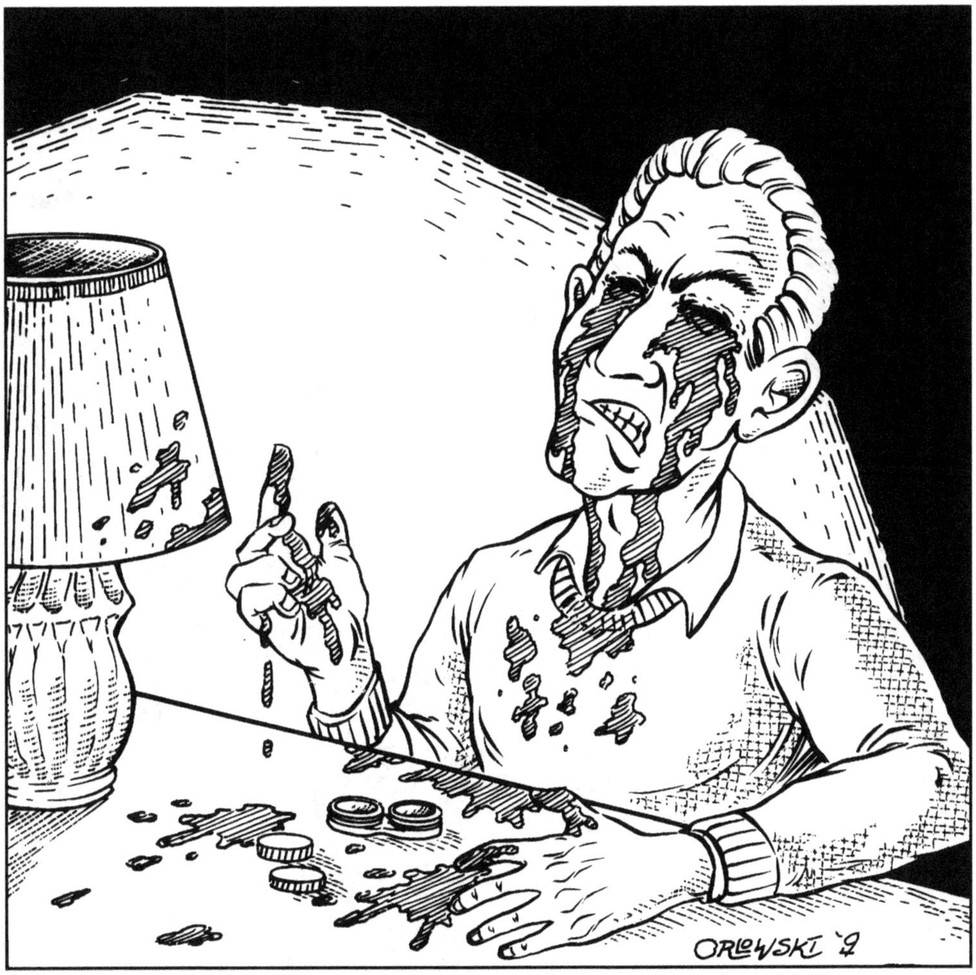
ORLOWSKI '9

Philip sat down to take his
contacts out, and after hours and hours of
scraping his eyes until they bled, he realized
he hadn't even worn them that day.

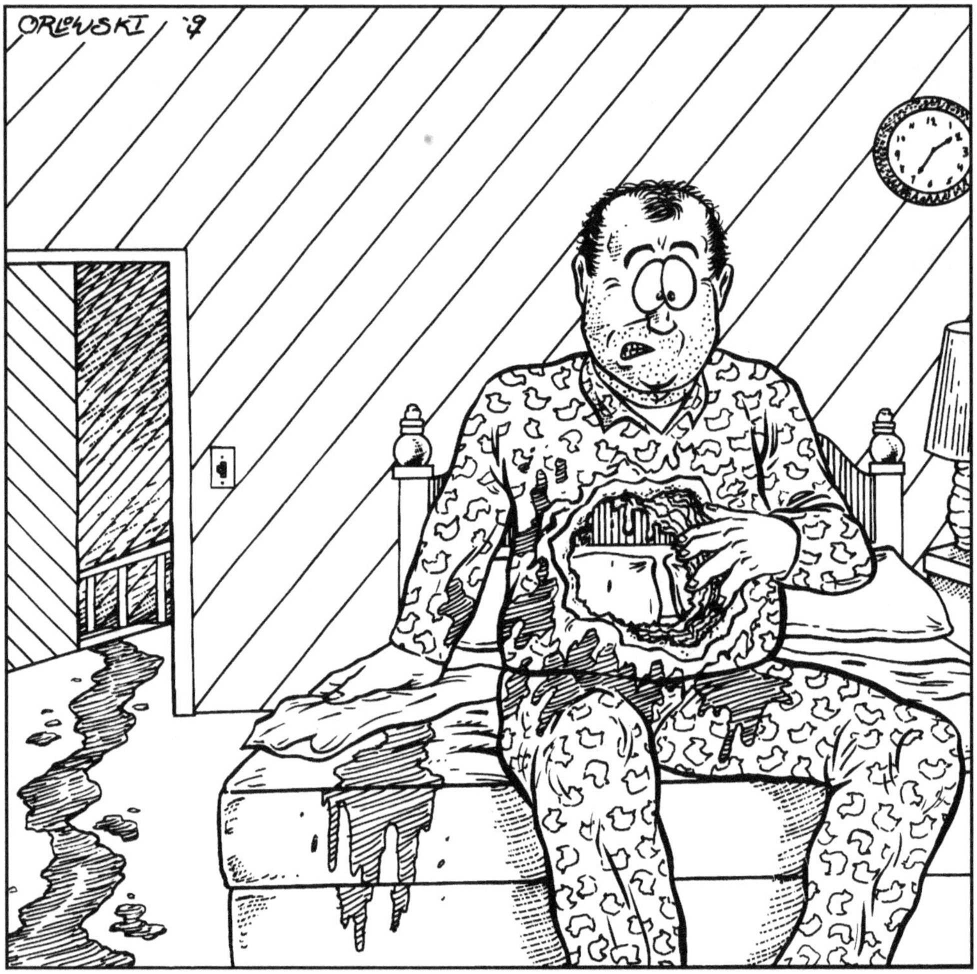
ORLOWSKI '9

Charles awoke to discover that
once again his stomach had eaten its way
out and was now probably running loose and
terrorizing the neighborhood.

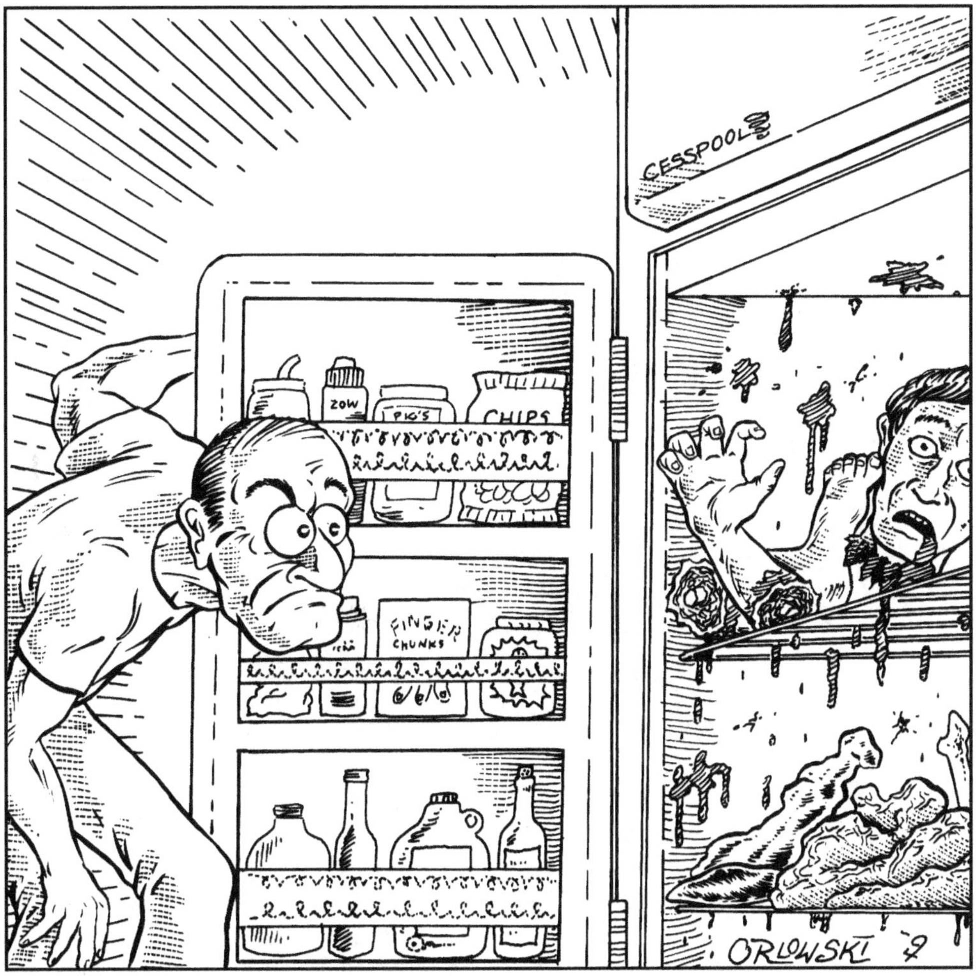
CESSPOOL
ZOW
PIG'S
CHIPS
FINGER CHUNKS
ORLOWSKI

Upon opening the fridge, Don was shocked and furious that his wife had stocked the shelves with body parts and major organs, but had forgotten the milk.

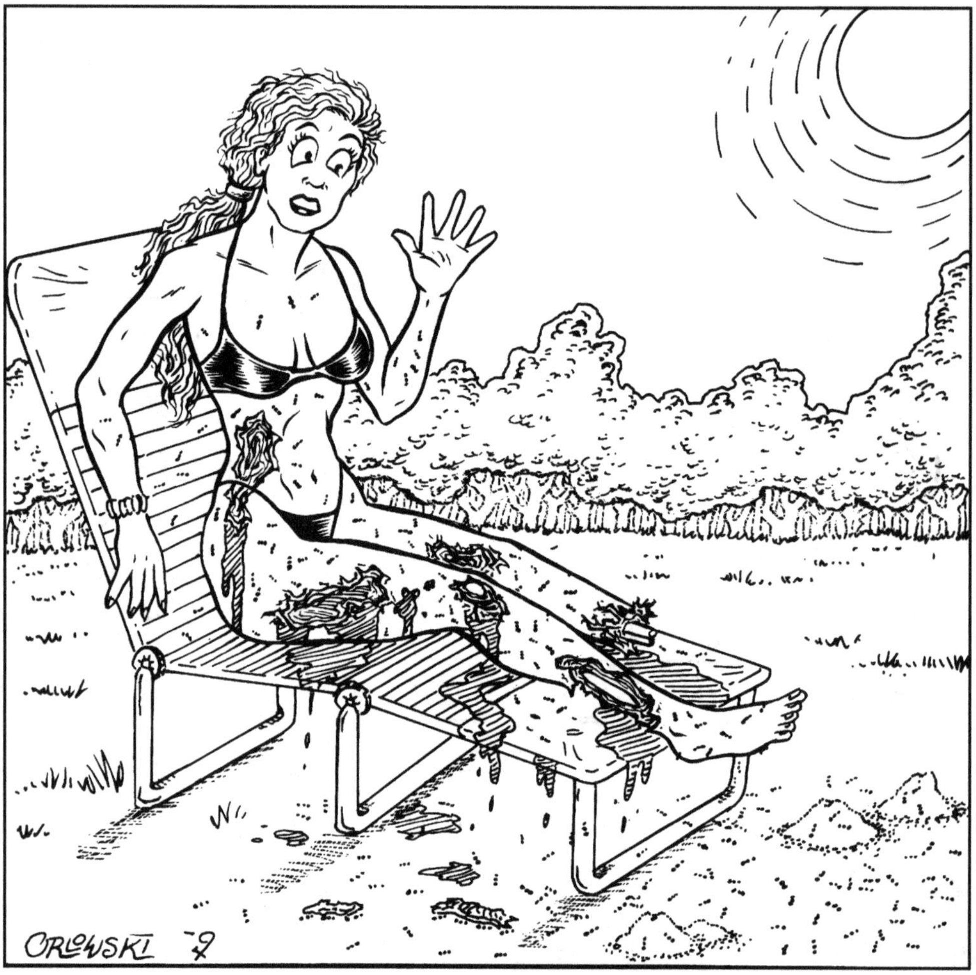
ORLOWSKI

Opening her eyes, Debbie found herself in the process of being eaten alive by ants, and was concerned that the wounds, once healed, would tan evenly.

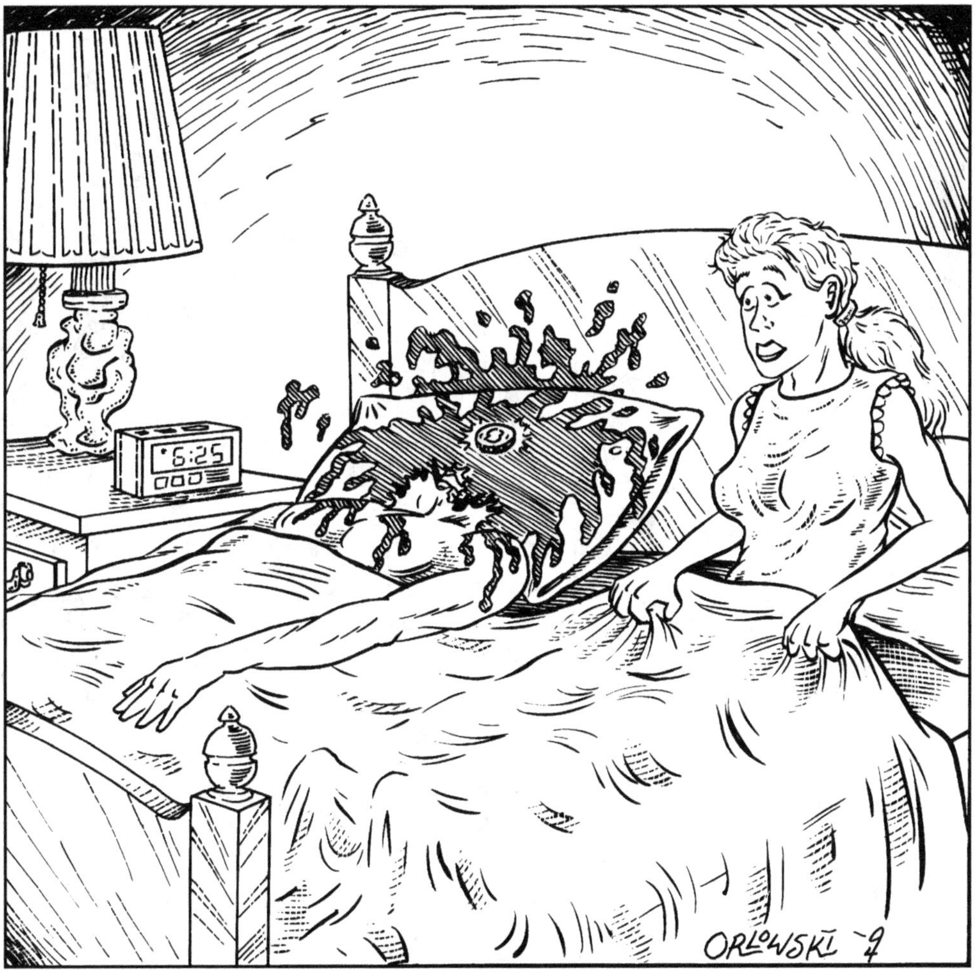
6:25
ORLOWSKI

Melanie awoke to find her husband's head violently removed, and upon seeing the shiny, new quarter, realized there really was truth in those childhood tales of the Head Fairy.

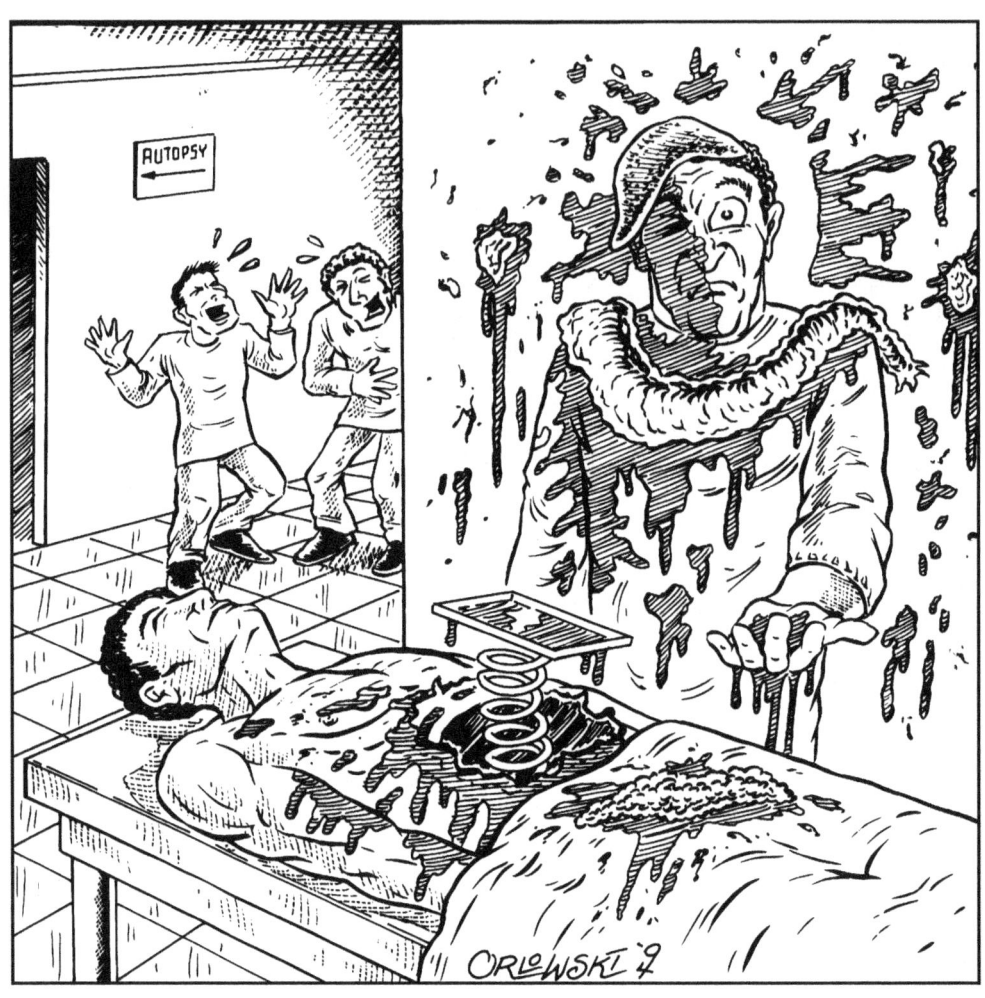

Being the new guy, Joel had to put up with many of the other coroners' practical jokes, his least favorite being the "Sproing-O-Guts 3000".

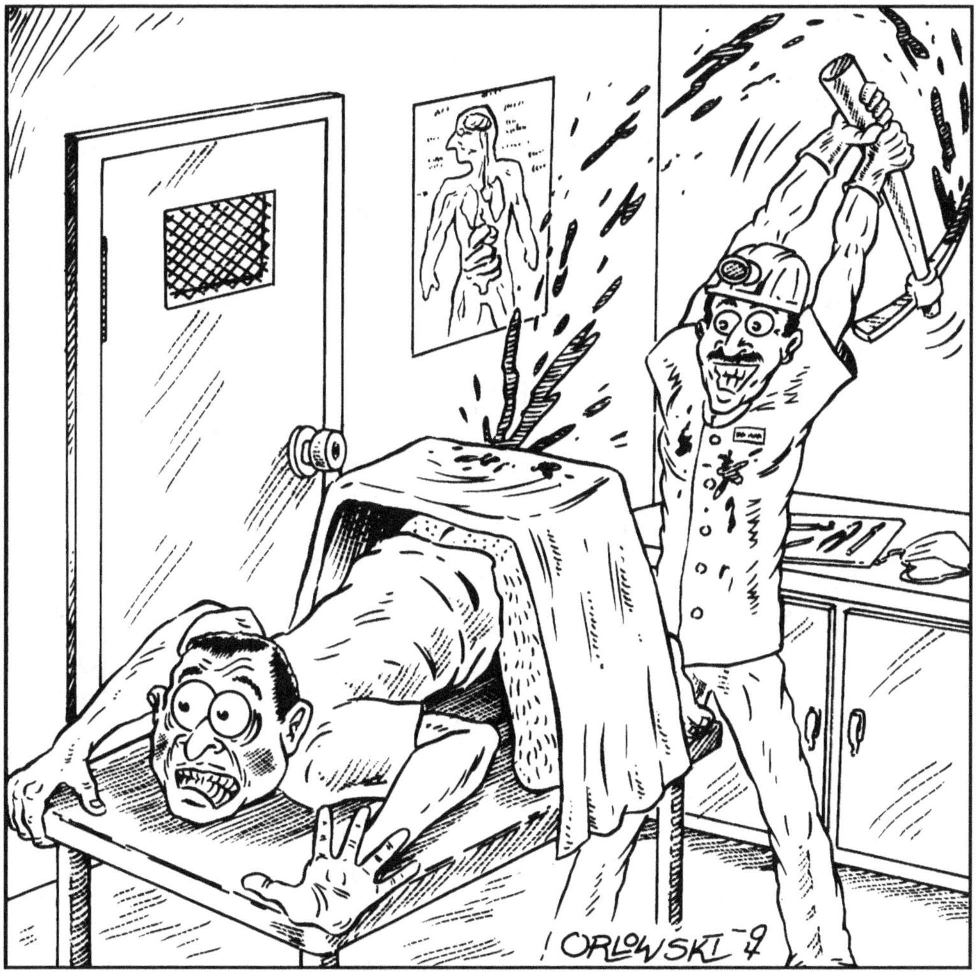
ORLOWSKI

On January 21st, while in the middle of hemorrhoidal surgery, renowned proctologist Dr. Roberts experienced an unexpected flashback to his days in the coal mines.

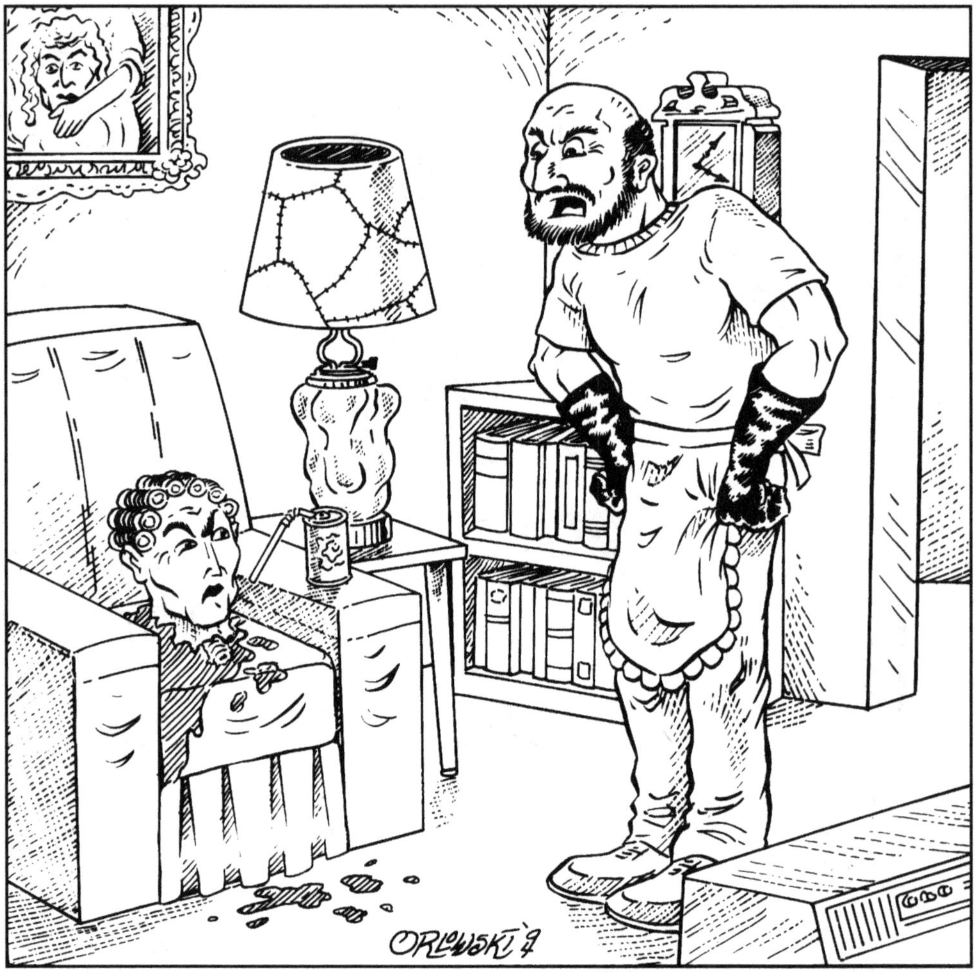
ORLOWSKI '9

"Whine, whine, whine! That's all you do! You think it's easy being married to a severed head? 'Move me here, clean up this blood, feed me, fix my hair!' and not to mention only having one sexual position!"

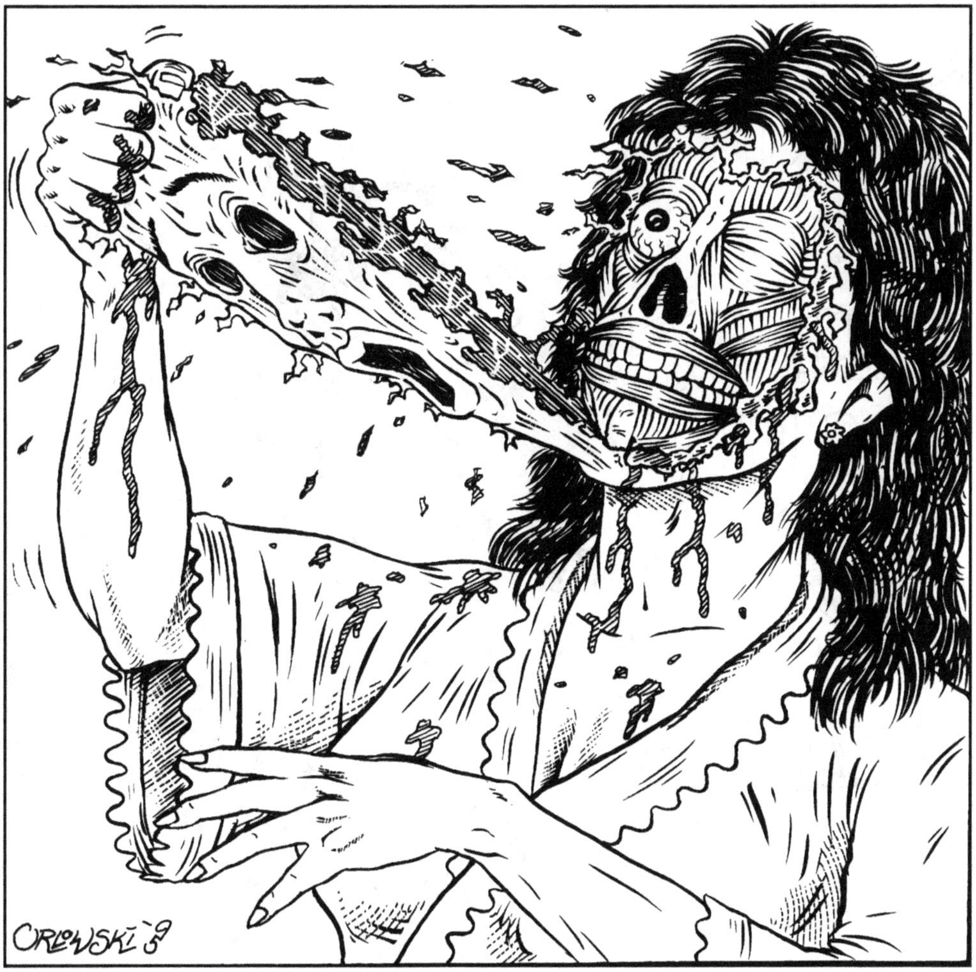
ORLOWSKI

It was only after struggling through
the slow, painful removal of her entire face that
Nora realized how similar the tubes of mudmask
and extra-strength glue were.

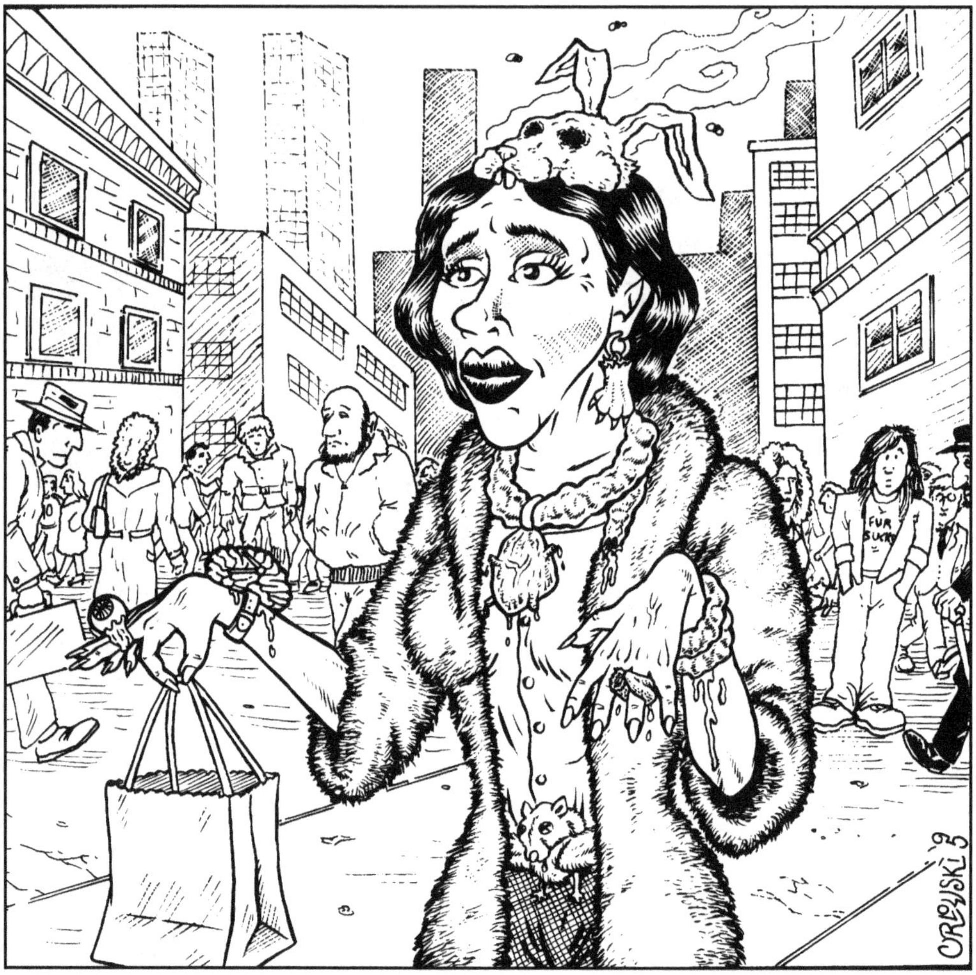
FUR

It is foreseen in the future that
people who wear fur will be further disillusioned
and believe wearing the organs and scraps of animals
will look better than their pelts alone.

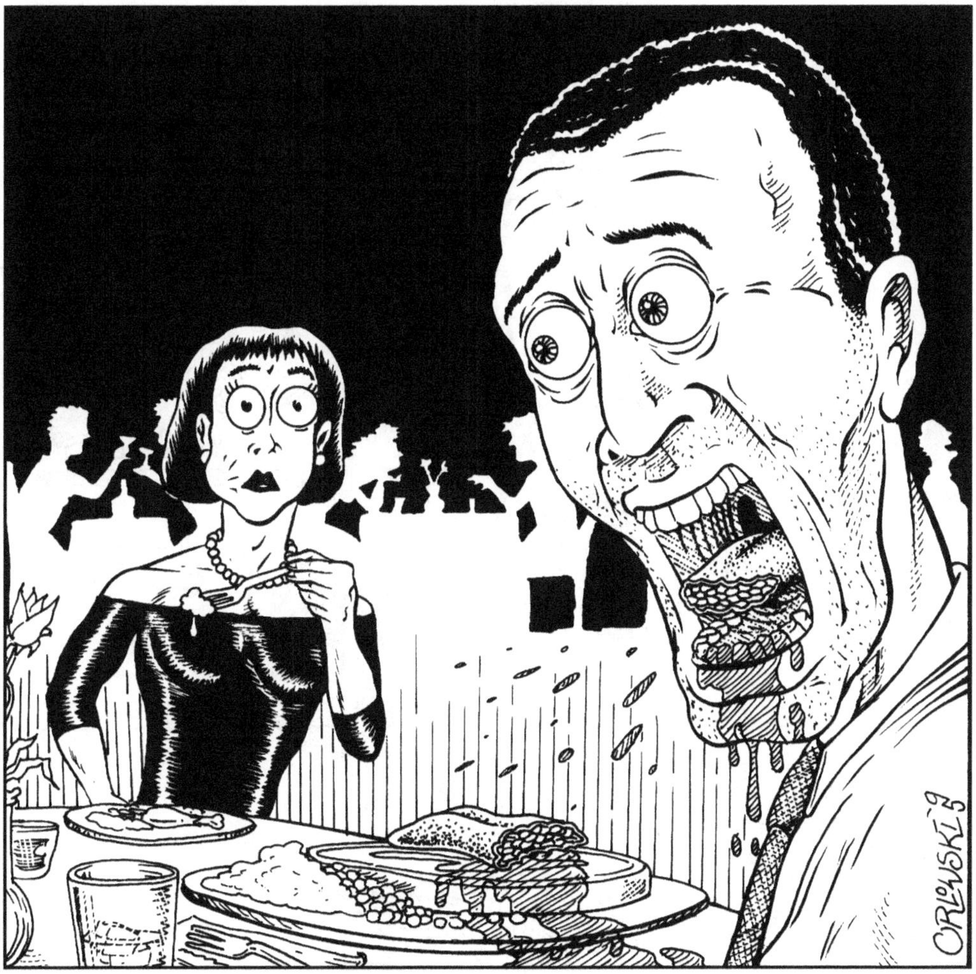
ORLOWSKI

Bad Timing Number 43:
"Dana will you"-*crunch*-"Mahee me?
Wih yuh mahee me? Foh clyin' oht lod, ahm
tyin' ta ass yuh ta mahee me!"

Without thinking, Professor Stevens
missed the soda can and grabbed the hydrochloric acid,
instantly dissolving himself from mouth to nether regions,
and permanently quenching his thirst.

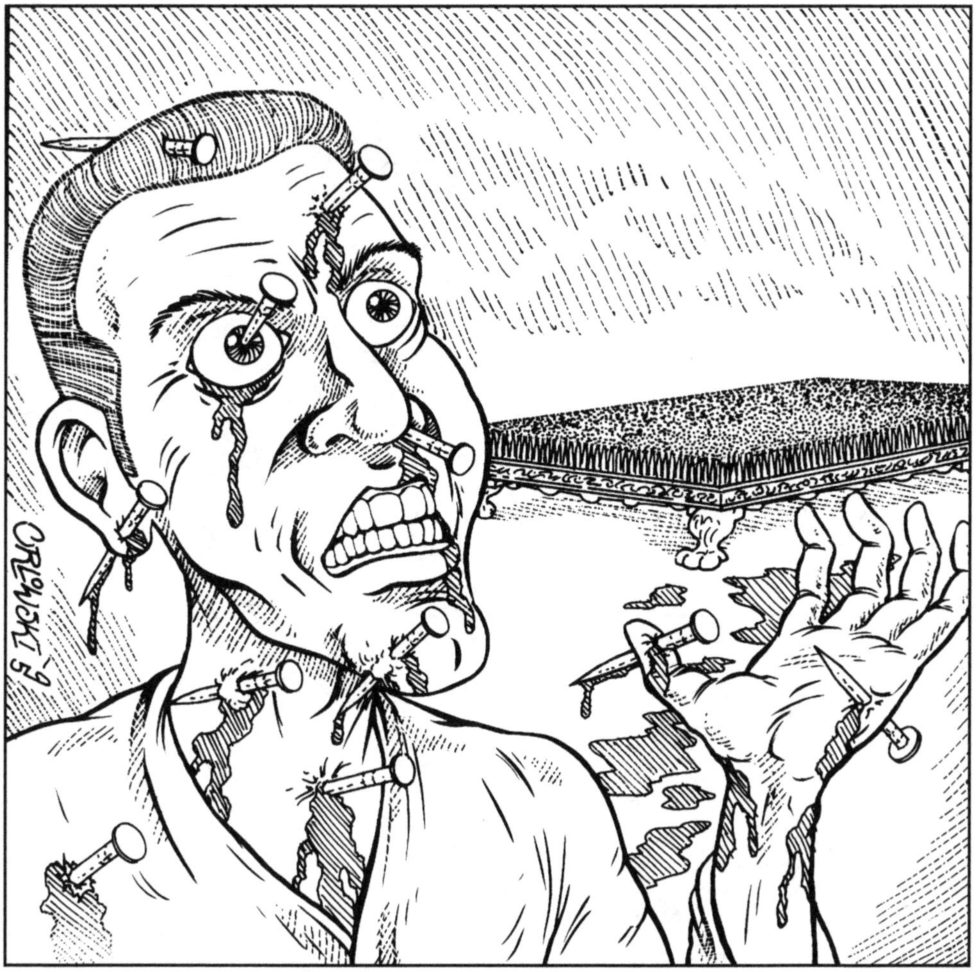
ORLOWSKI '09

For Thad, taking up yoga
was great, even lying on the bed of nails
was great, unfortunately, falling asleep and
tossing and turning was not.

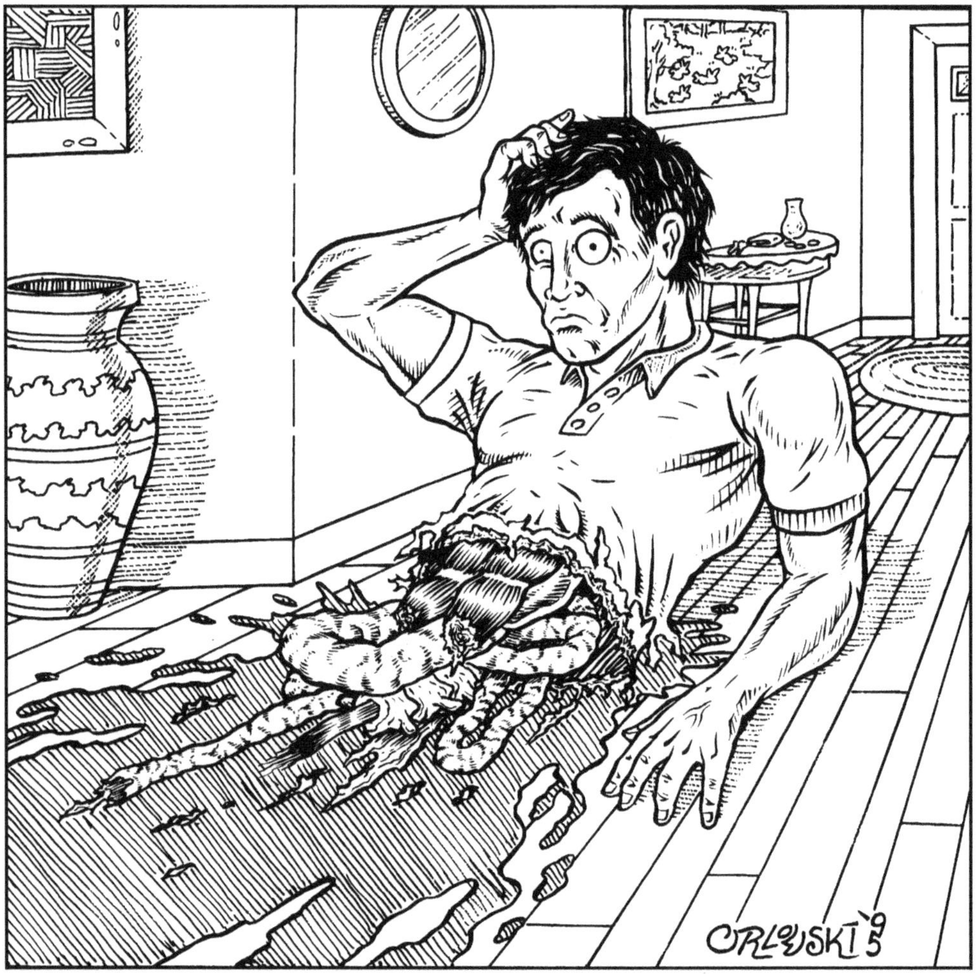
ORLOWSKI '95

Nick repeatedly went over his day,
mentally retracing his steps since morning,
but for the life of him he couldn't remember
where he'd left his lower half.

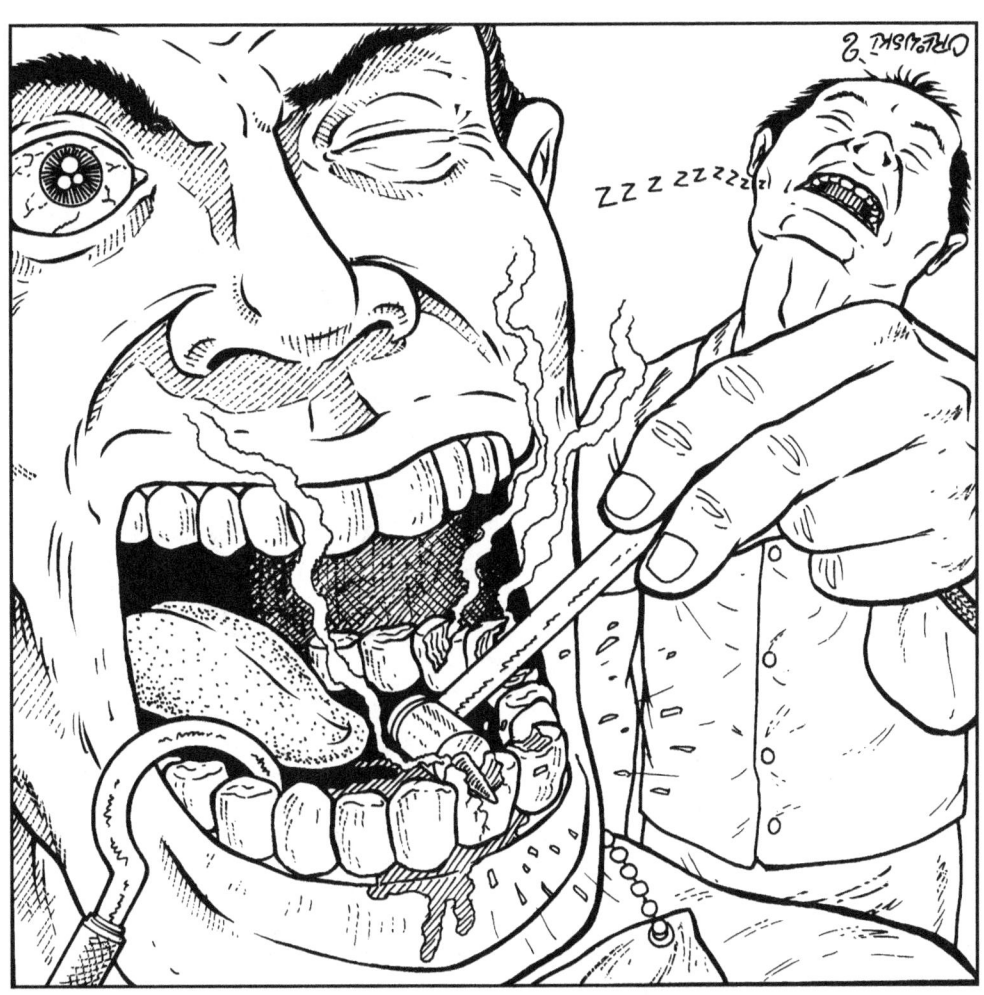

Joe decided he had reached the point where his trust in his dentist's professionalism must be put aside in light of Dr. Winter's chronic narcolepsy.

When Melvin set out to break the world record for flagpole sitting, nobody informed him it required a perch of some kind.

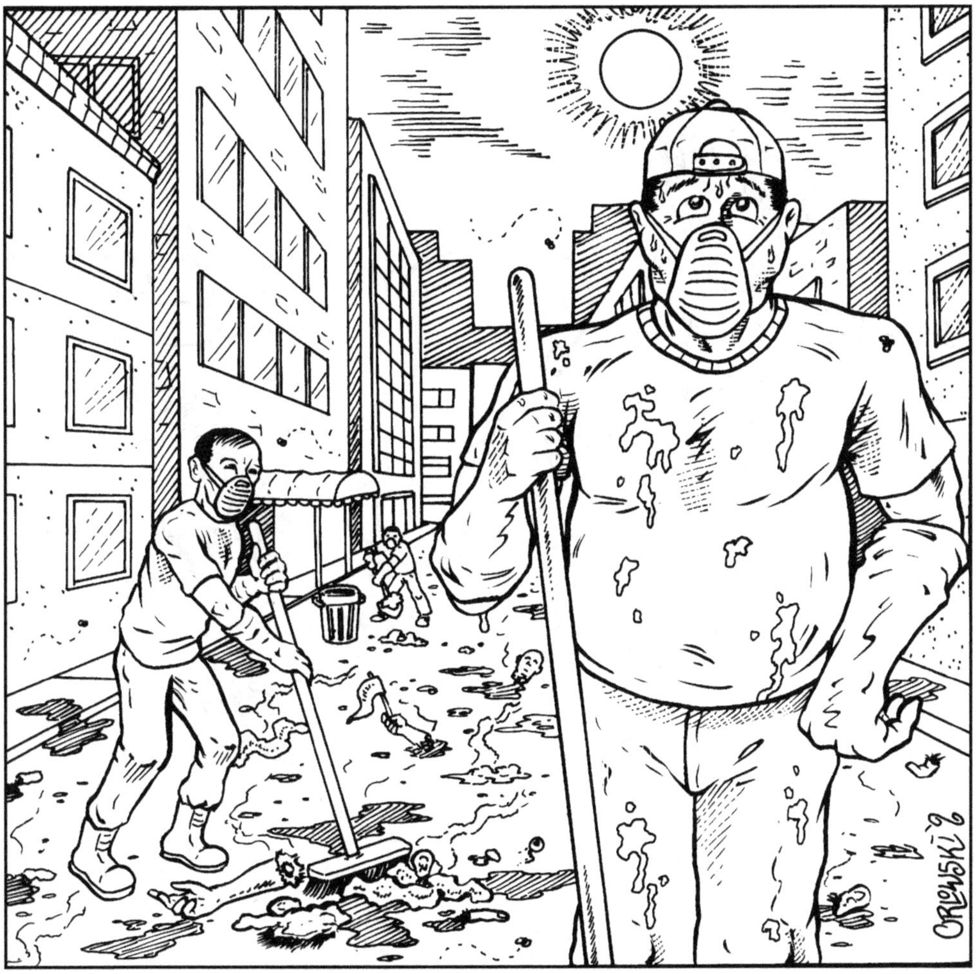
ORLEWSKI '02

Brad had been cleaning up after parades
for years, but the one he feared the most, the one
that no way, no how, should be held in the heat of July,
was the Annual Leper's Day Parade.

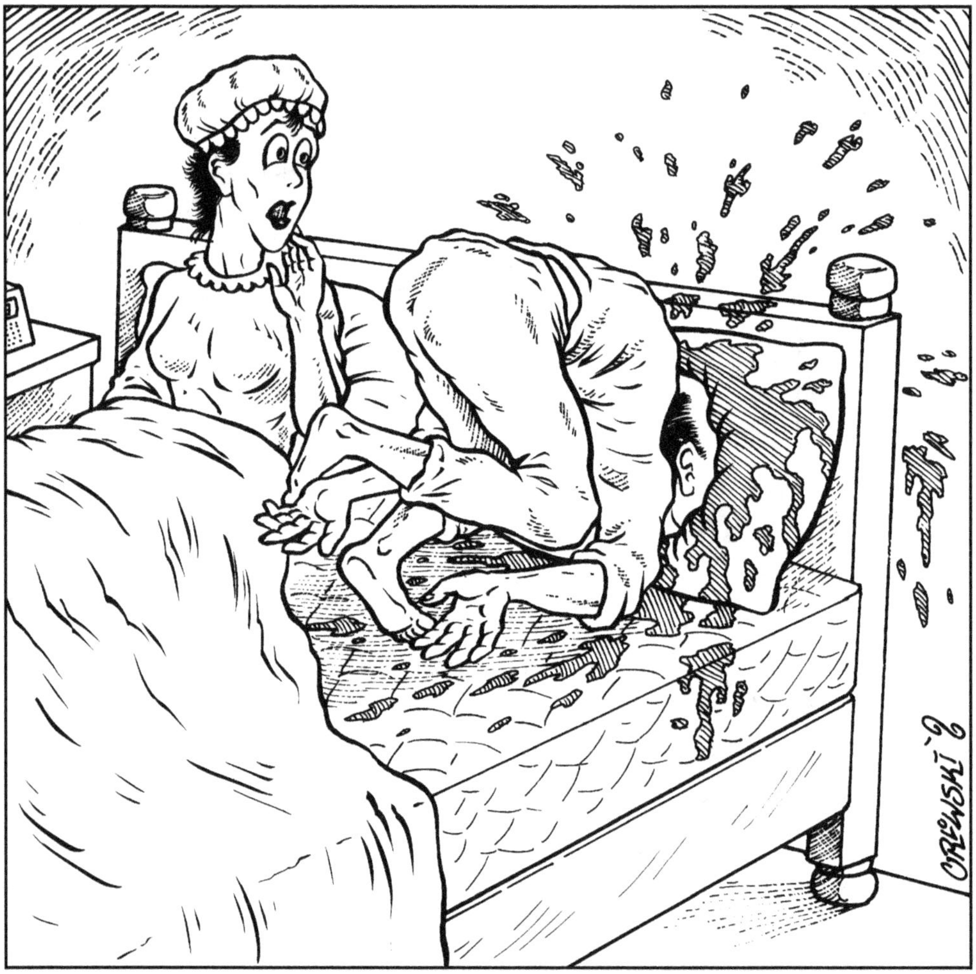
ORLOWSKI '09

For years Mrs. Hordt knew her husband had reoccuring dreams of being a flying insect, and upon waking she knew he had finally met up with a windshield.

Nothing in the monsters' long, tortured existence could ruin the joy of the birth of their offspring, except maybe the assembly required.

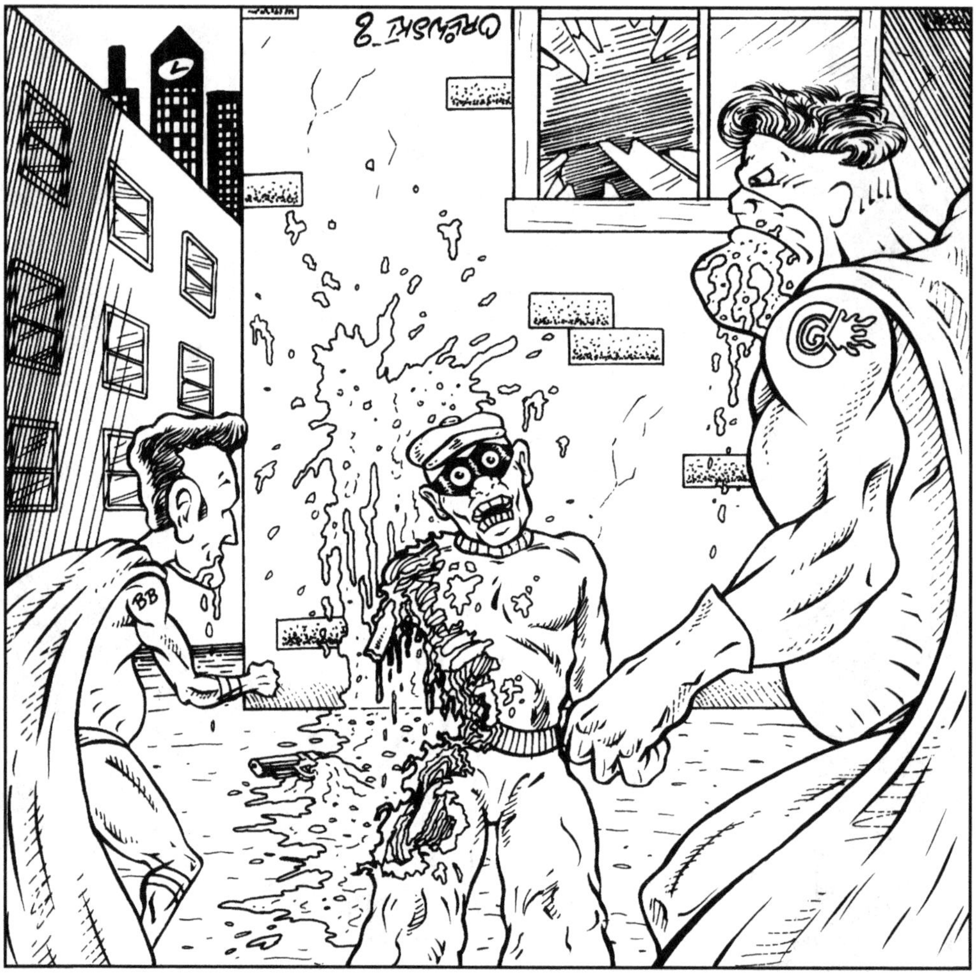
BB

Fear leaps into the hearts of
criminals everywhere when Captain Gastric and
Bile Boy, the Daring Duodenum, burst onto the scene
spewing their rousing battlecry,
"It's Chyme Time!!"

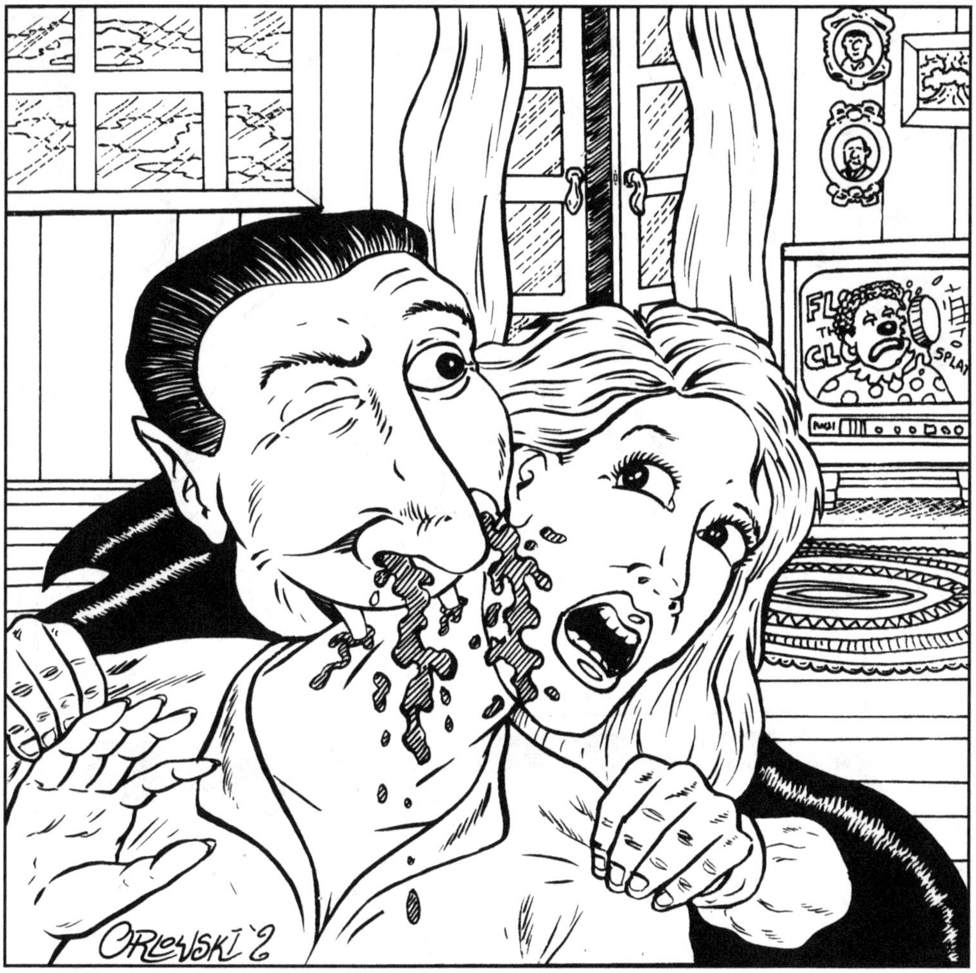
SPLAT

It was a total embarassment
to his professional and morbid image
when the count snarfed blood out
his nose while on the job.

Harry never thought he was any
good in bed, and though he'd always tried to impress,
he never imagined he could achieve what men have
been claiming to do for centuries.

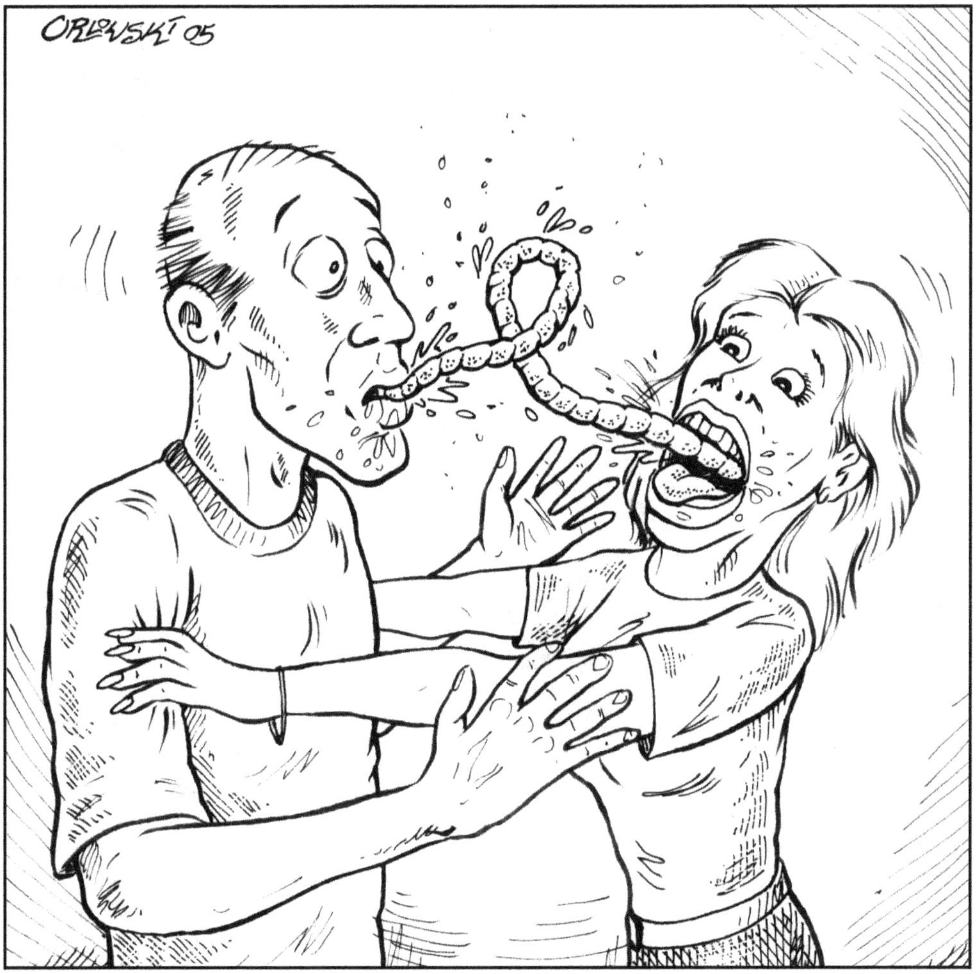
ORLOWSKI 05

Ted had learned to coexist
with his tapeworm and had few issues with it,
but he drew the line when it could smell
food on his date's breath.

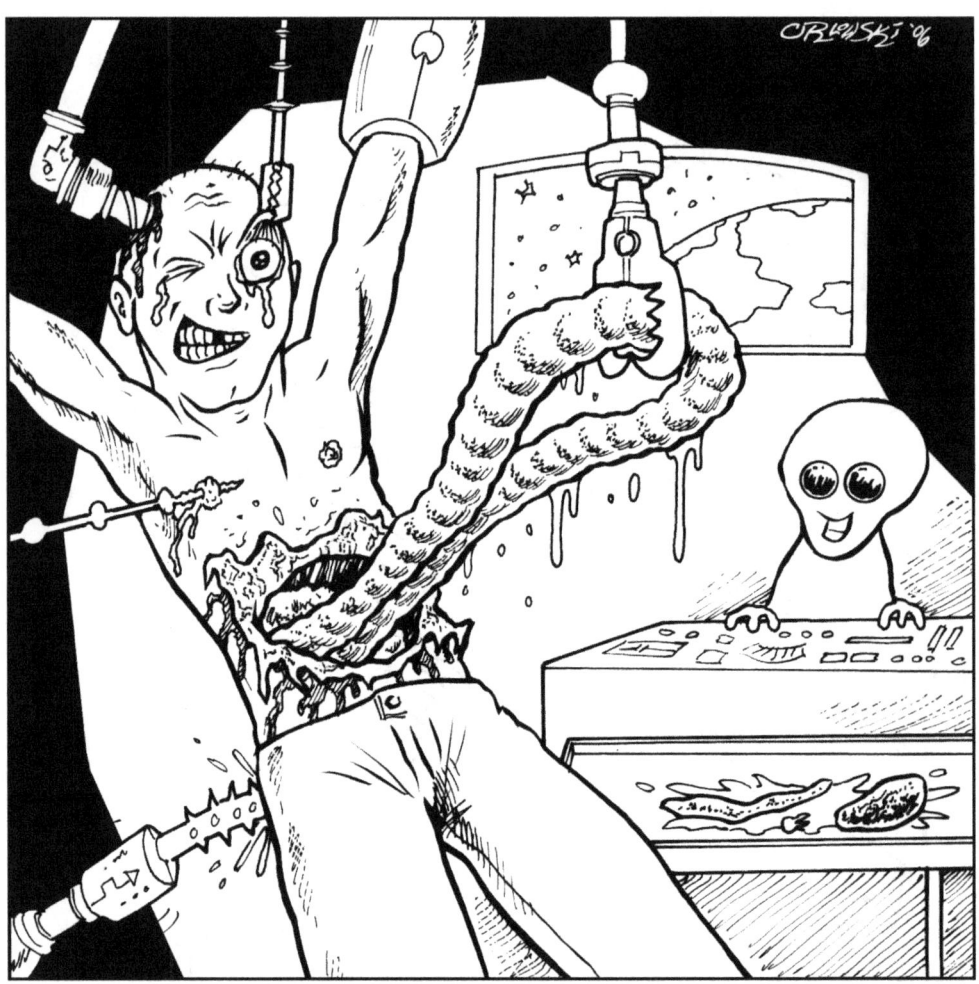

As the alien tortured him and
violently prodded and probed his every orifice,
Ed couldn't help but think about the money he would
make off of the book and movie deals.

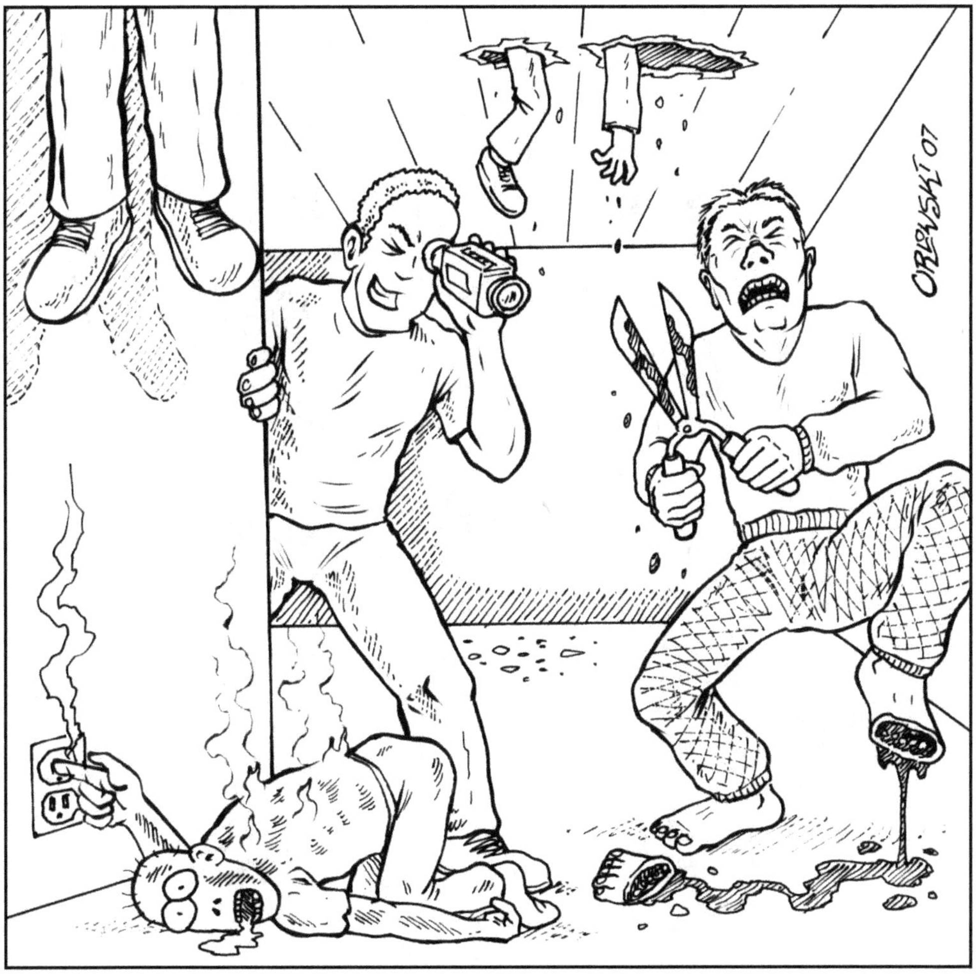
ORLOWSKI '07

Henry risked the life and limb of his family and damaged most of his home in his obsessive pursuit of the grand prize on America's Wackiest Home Video.

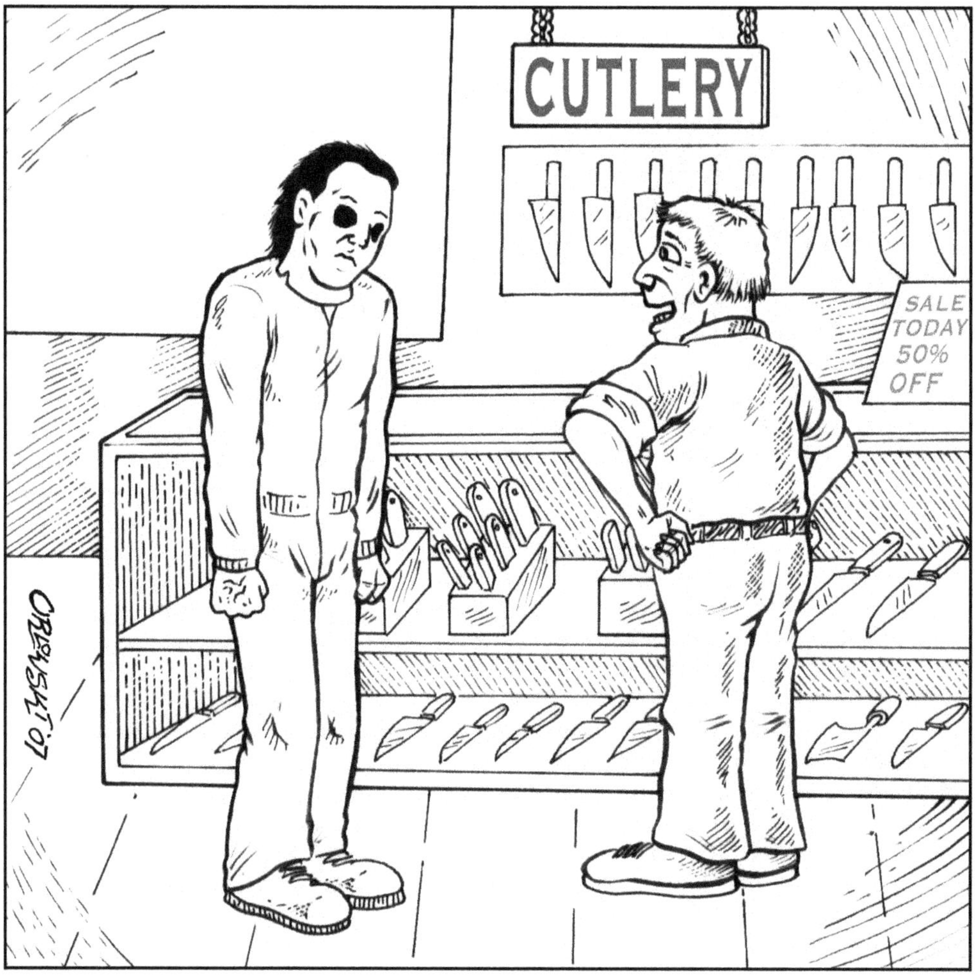
CUTLERY
SALE TODAY 50% OFF

Stupid Question Number 23:
"Welcome to Knife World,
see anything you like?"

ORLOWSKI '07
THIRD ATTEMPT! WRONG PIN NUMBER!

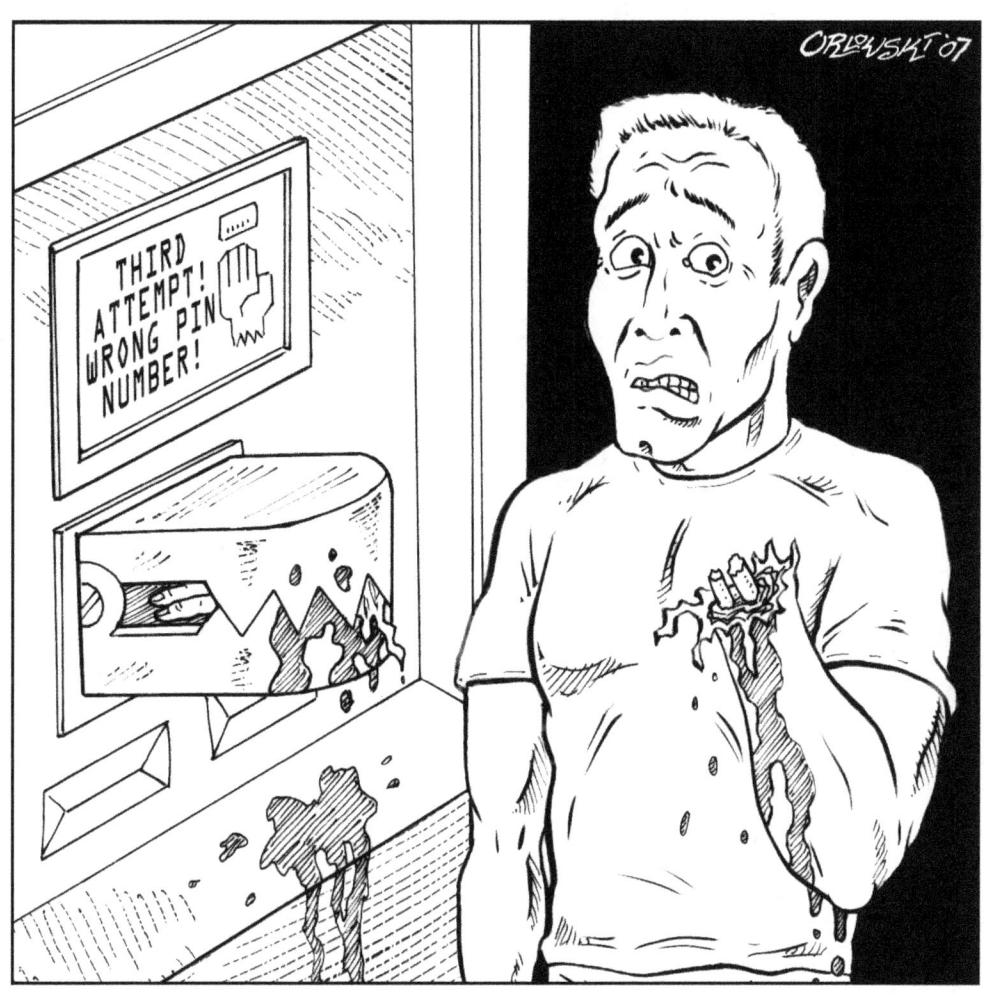

Stan obviously missed reading
the disclaimer sent to him about his
bank stiffening the penalties on incorrect
ATM pin numbers.

Hank knew he picked his nose too deeply and, moments after seeing the grey matter on his finger, he realized he'd lobotomized himself.

Not that Alice lacked faith in her husband's uneven history as a handyman, but she always kept the electrician and plumber on her speed dial, just below 9-1-1.

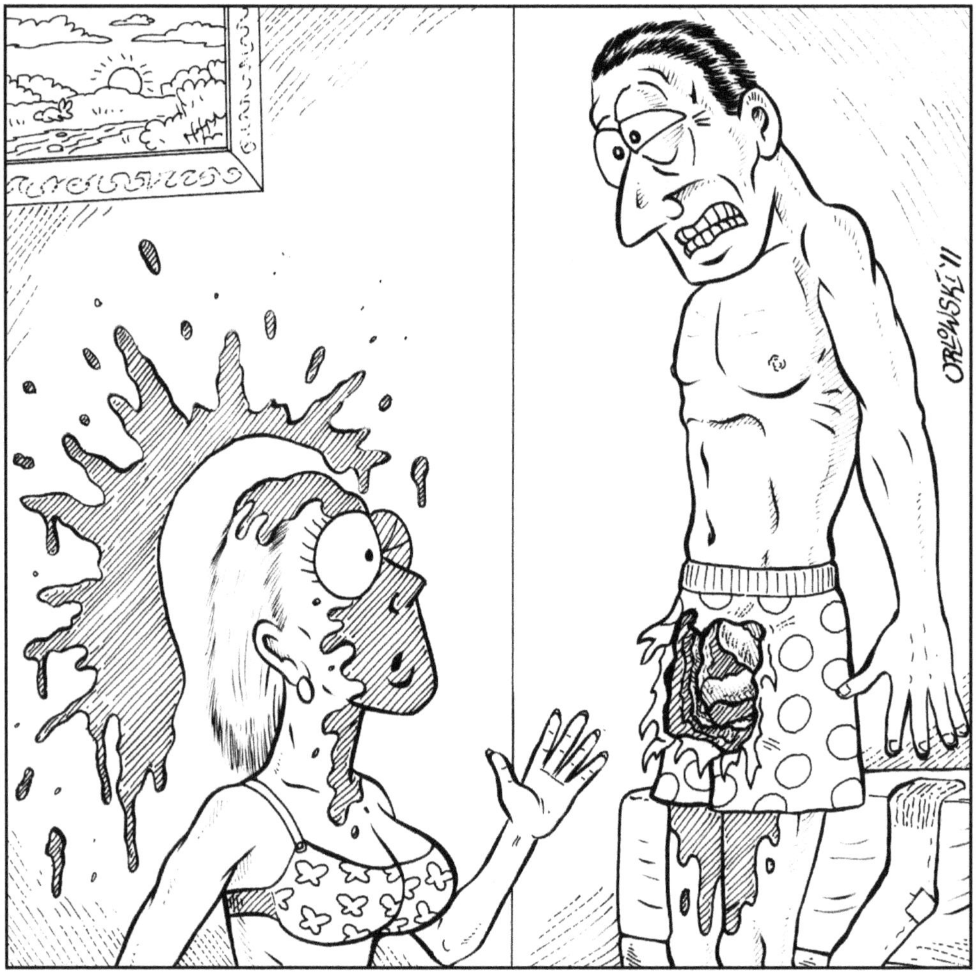
ORLOWSKI '11

Matt had never thought that in his
lifetime he'd get to sleep with a supermodel,
and being concerned with impressing her,
he took about five Viagra too many.

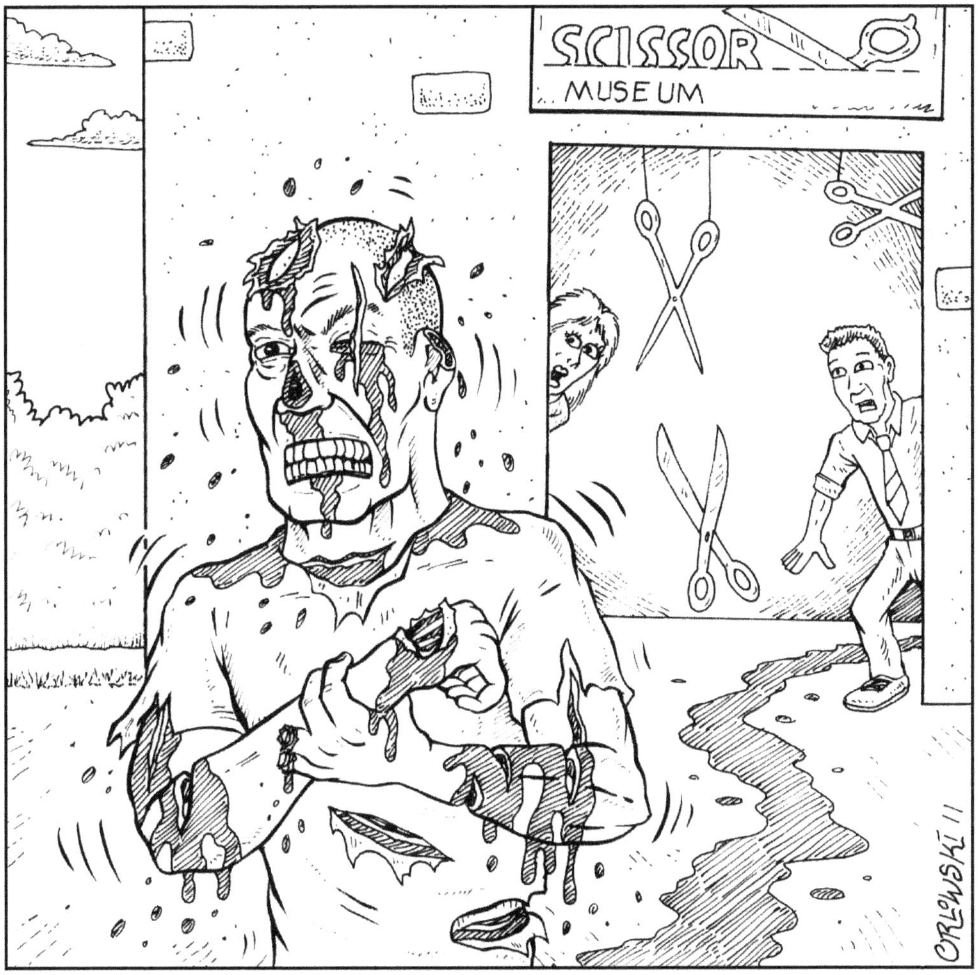
SCISSOR
MUSEUM
ORLOWSKI 11

Of all the field trips his school offered, of all the places he could have gone to, Palsy Paul regrettably decided the trip to the Scissor Museum was a good idea.

A die-hard fan for many years, Ronald discovered the health risks of two decades of doing the wave.

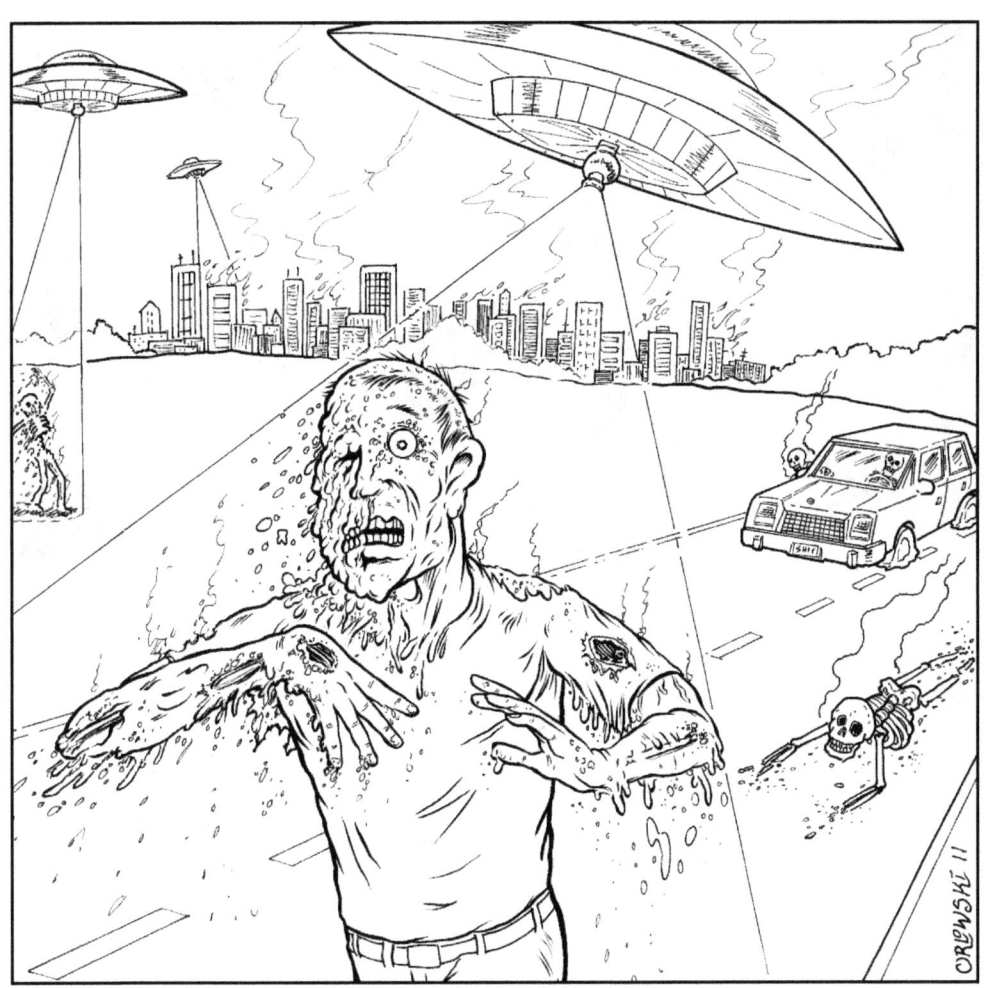

As the aliens destroyed the city and melted the skin off of Luke, he couldn't help but laugh at the newspaper headlines: "World being attacked by Uranus".

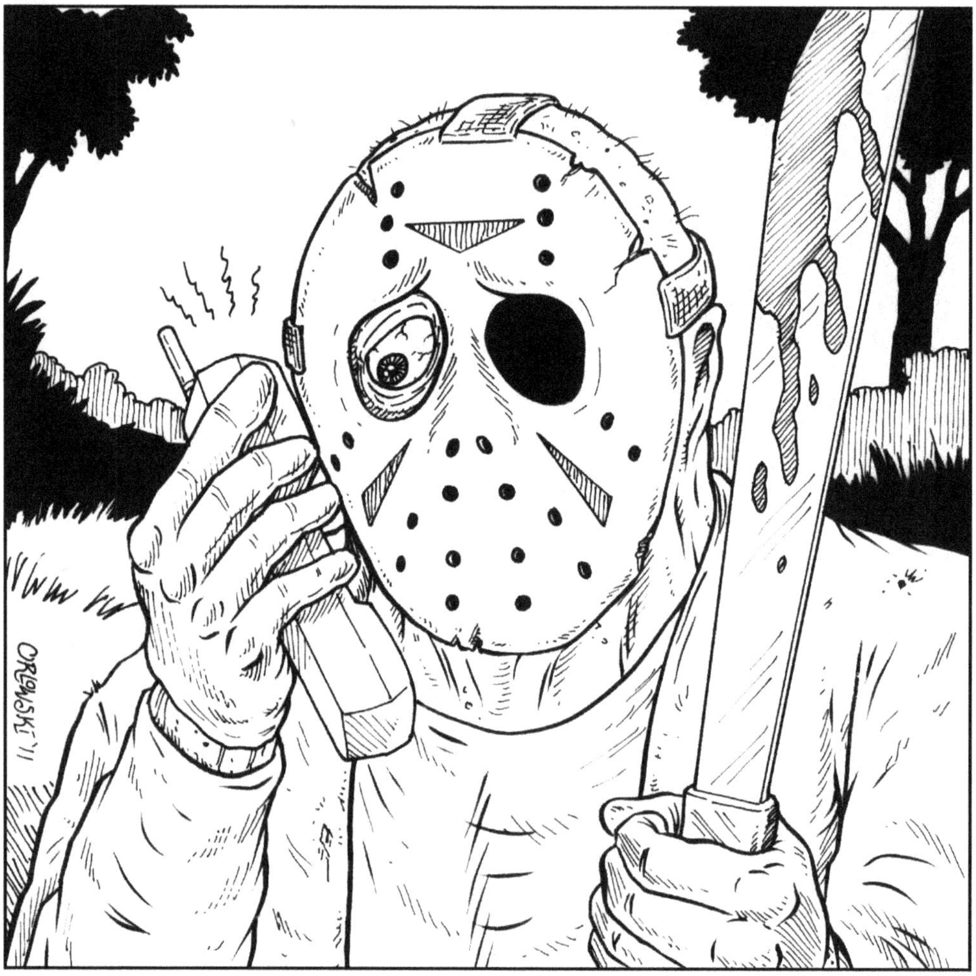
ORLOWSKI '11

*"Hello. You have reached the
Camp Crystal Lake automated phone line.
If you are calling about hours of operations,
please say 'yes'. If you wish to speak to a
counselor, say 'counselor'."*

SAFETY FIRST
PLEASE DON'T DIE!
ORLOWSKI '11

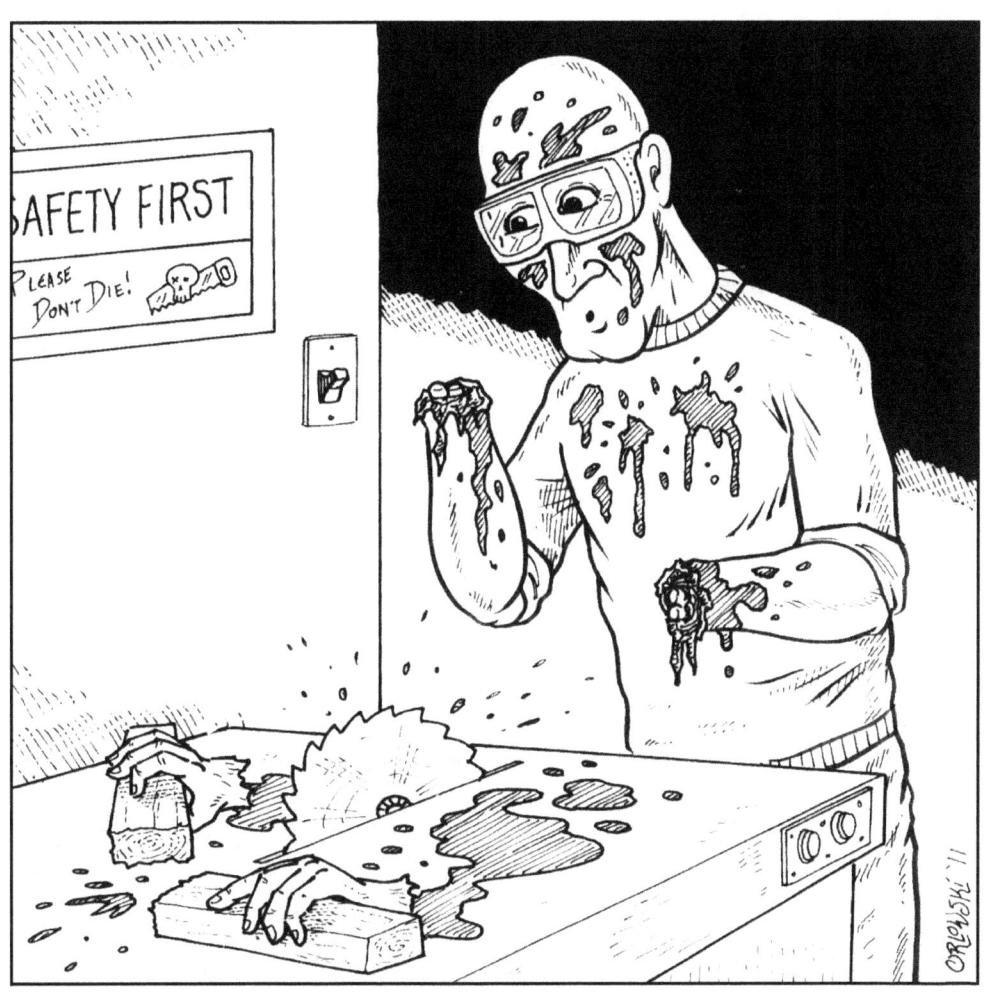

Neil was happy he at least
wore his safety goggles, but until
today had always thought paper cuts
were the most painful.

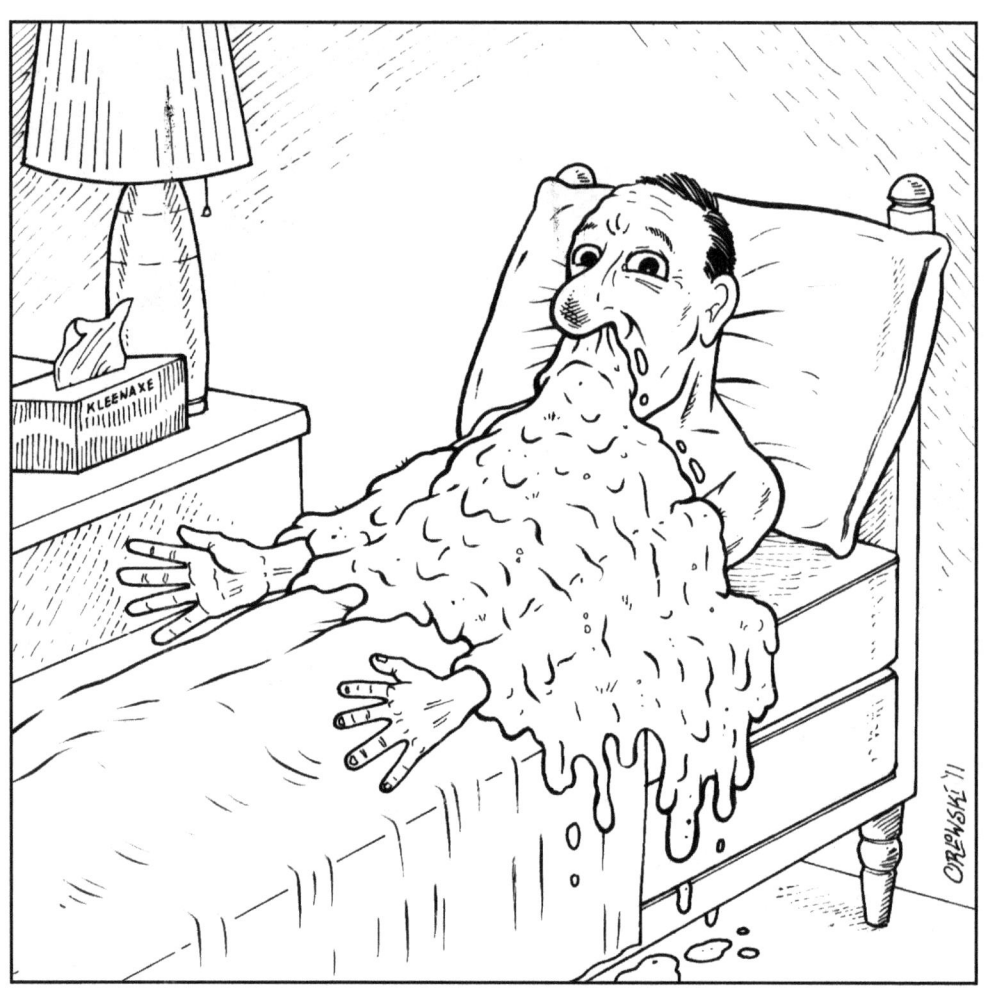

Lenny went to sleep with a minor cold and runny nose but never thought he'd wake up glued to the bed in an avalanche of dried snot.

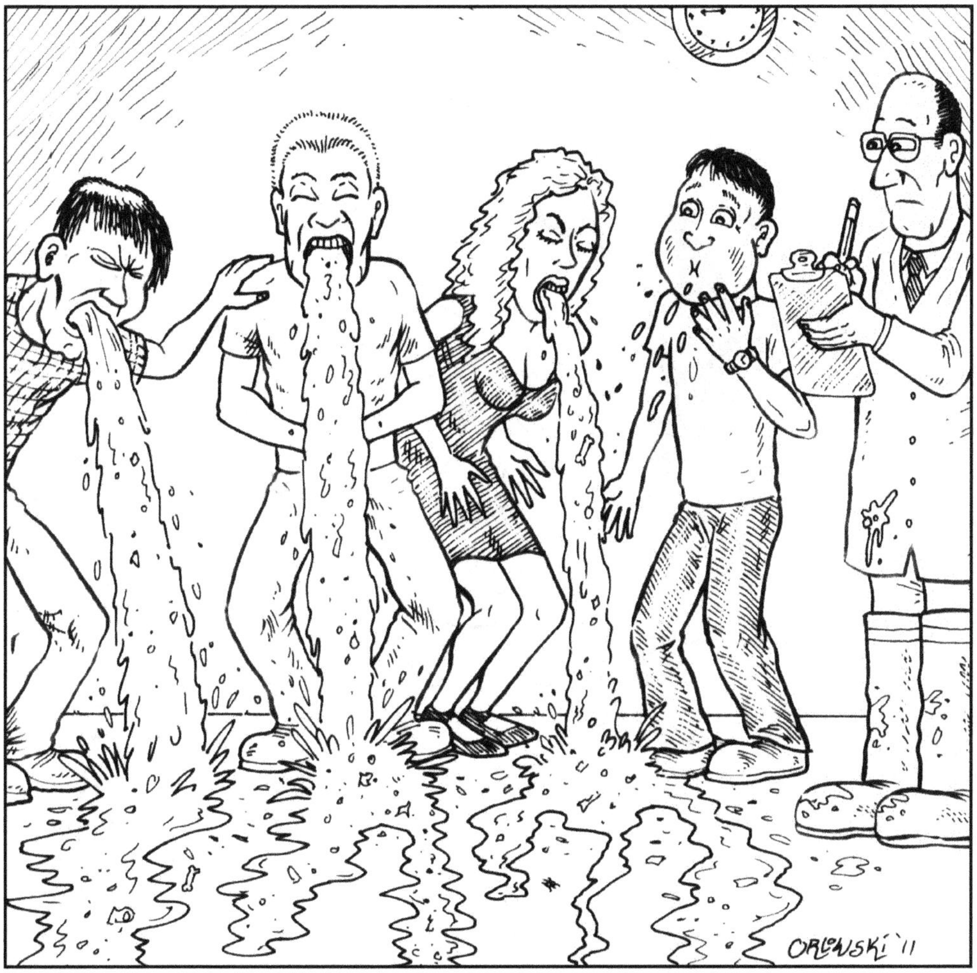
ORLOWSKI '11

It has been proven through
science and extensive research that vomiting
is far more contagious than yawning, especially
when fresh and super-chunky.

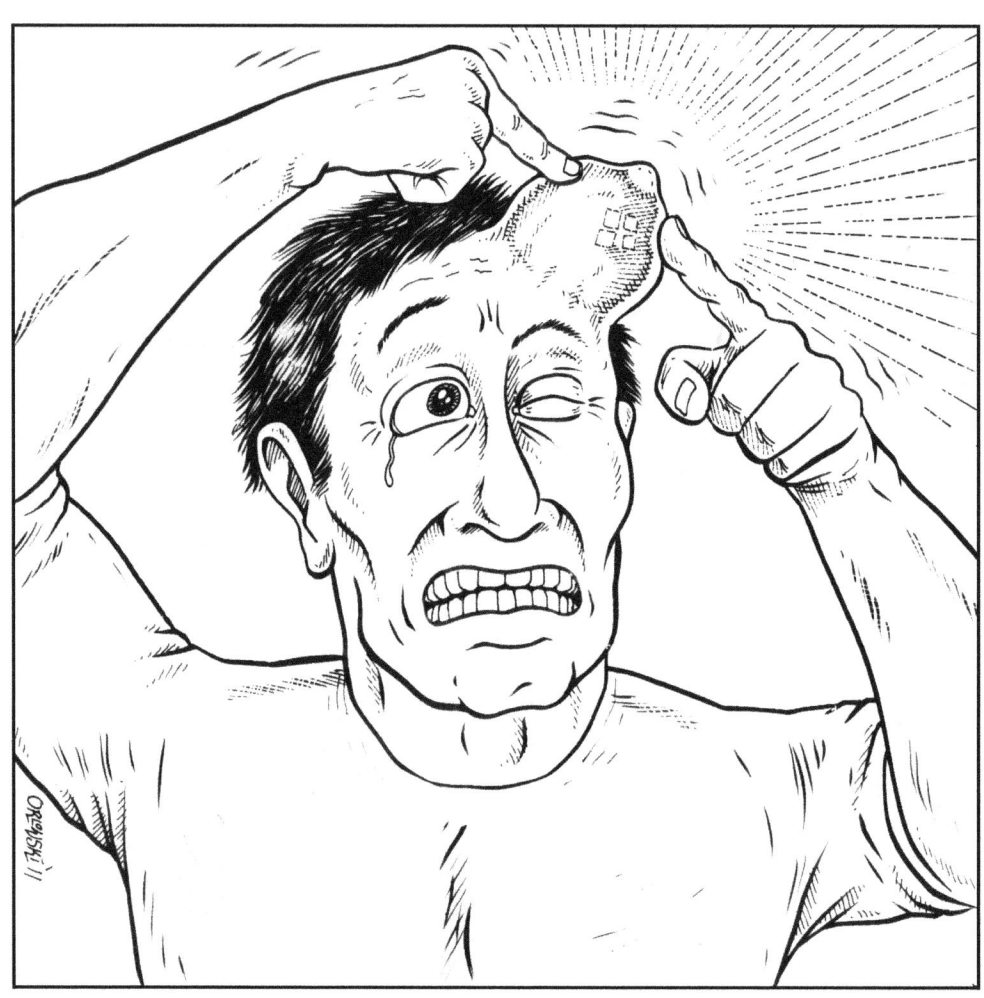

Having a big, wobbly, throbbing zit on his forehead was too tempting for Owen and he decided it was worth risking his life to pop it, he was found dead days later but his head was never recovered.

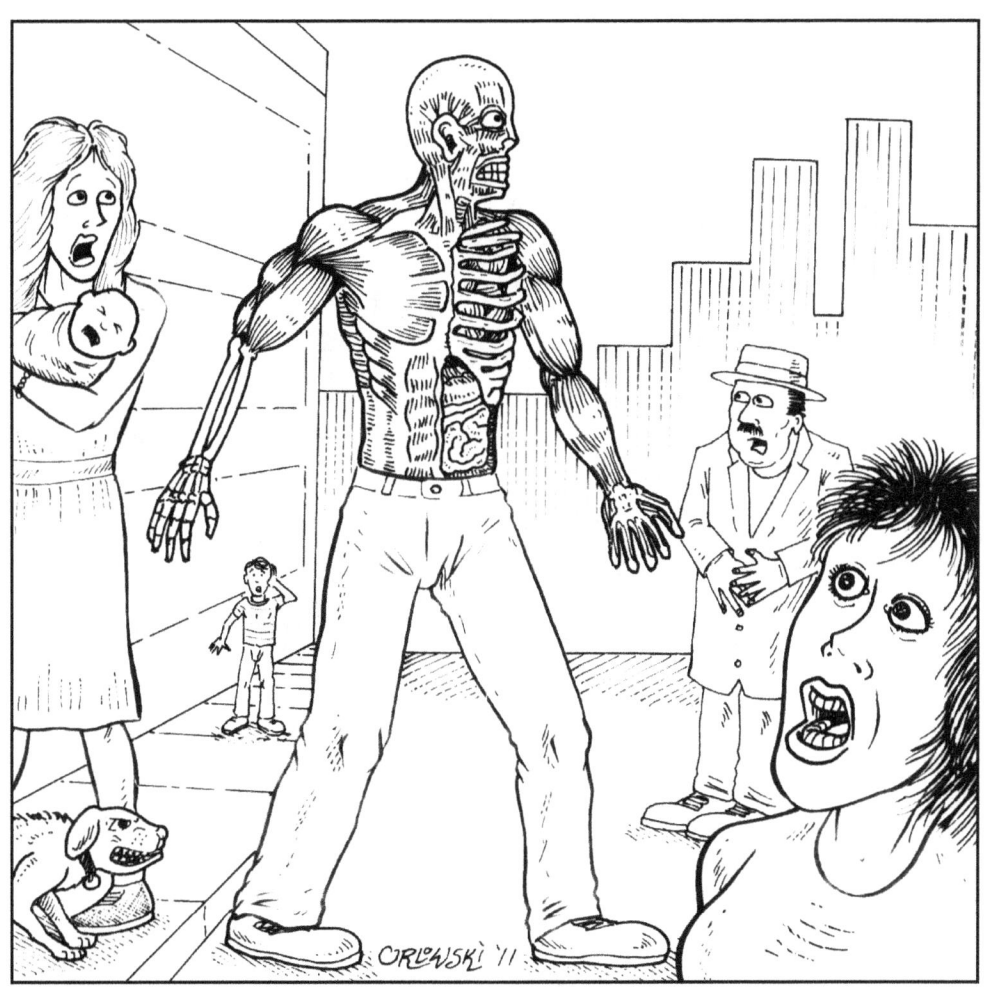

Stan had a successful career in modeling, he'd posed for every anatomy book ever made, but was never fully accepted by society.

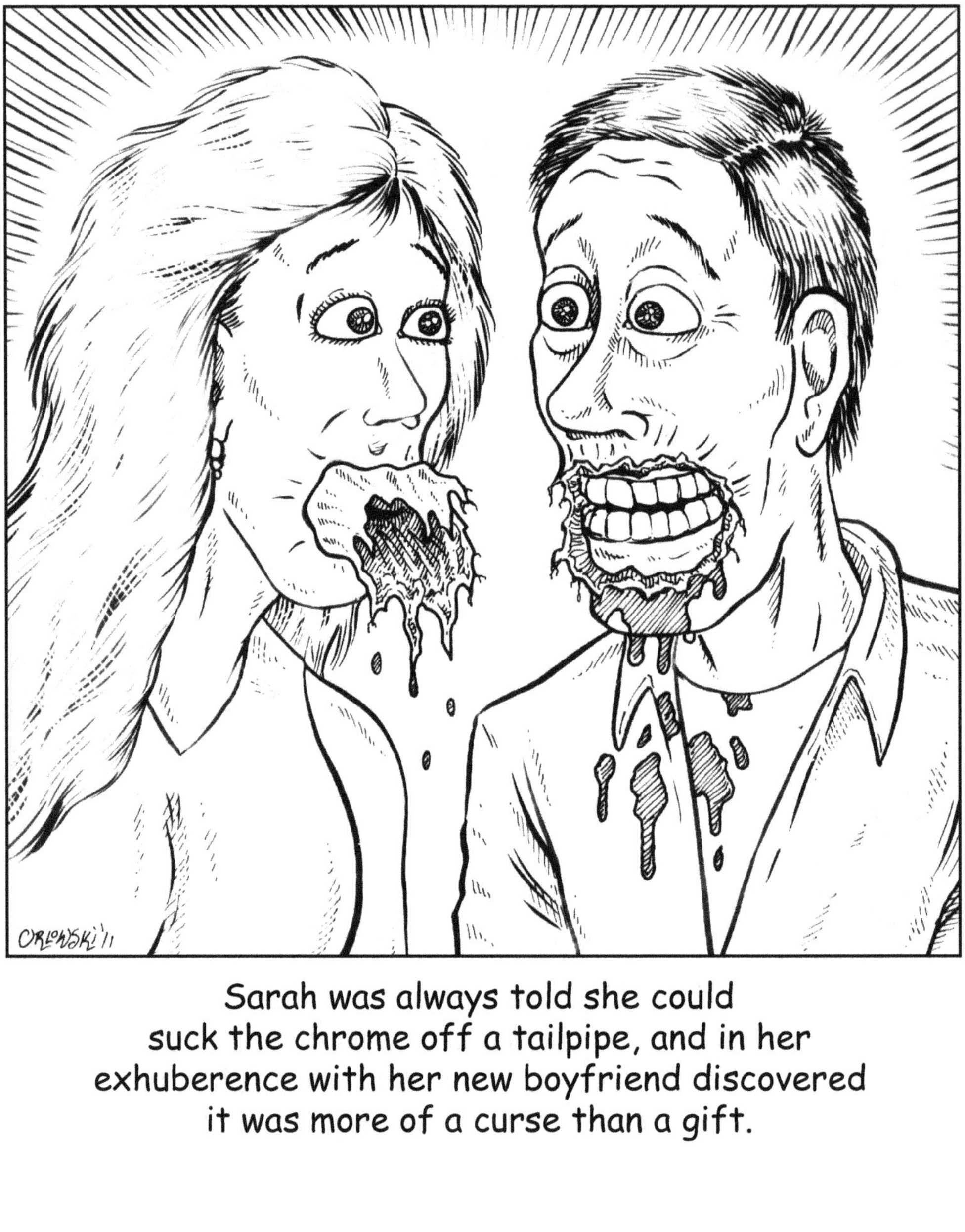
ORLOWSKI '11

Sarah was always told she could
suck the chrome off a tailpipe, and in her
exhuberence with her new boyfriend discovered
it was more of a curse than a gift.

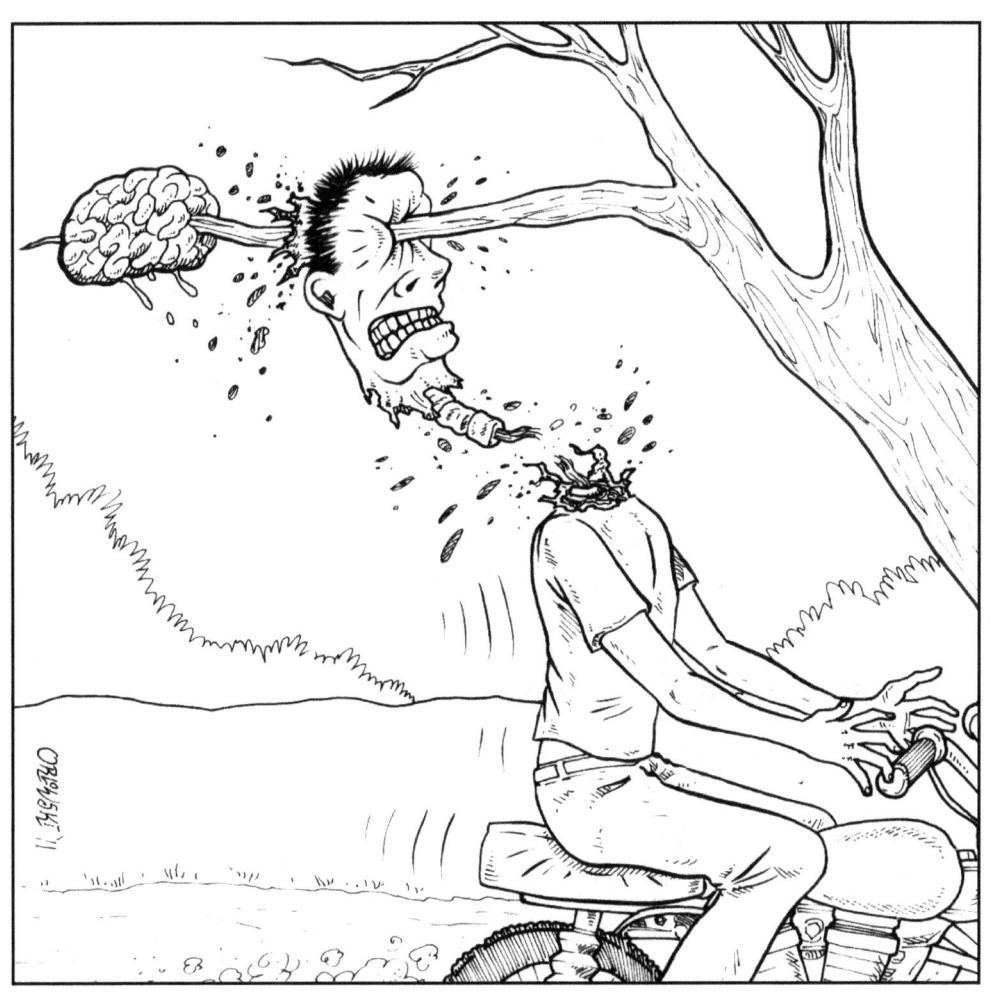

Hal had always thought the helmet law was silly and an affront to his civil liberties, that is until he became the poster boy, post-mortemly of course.

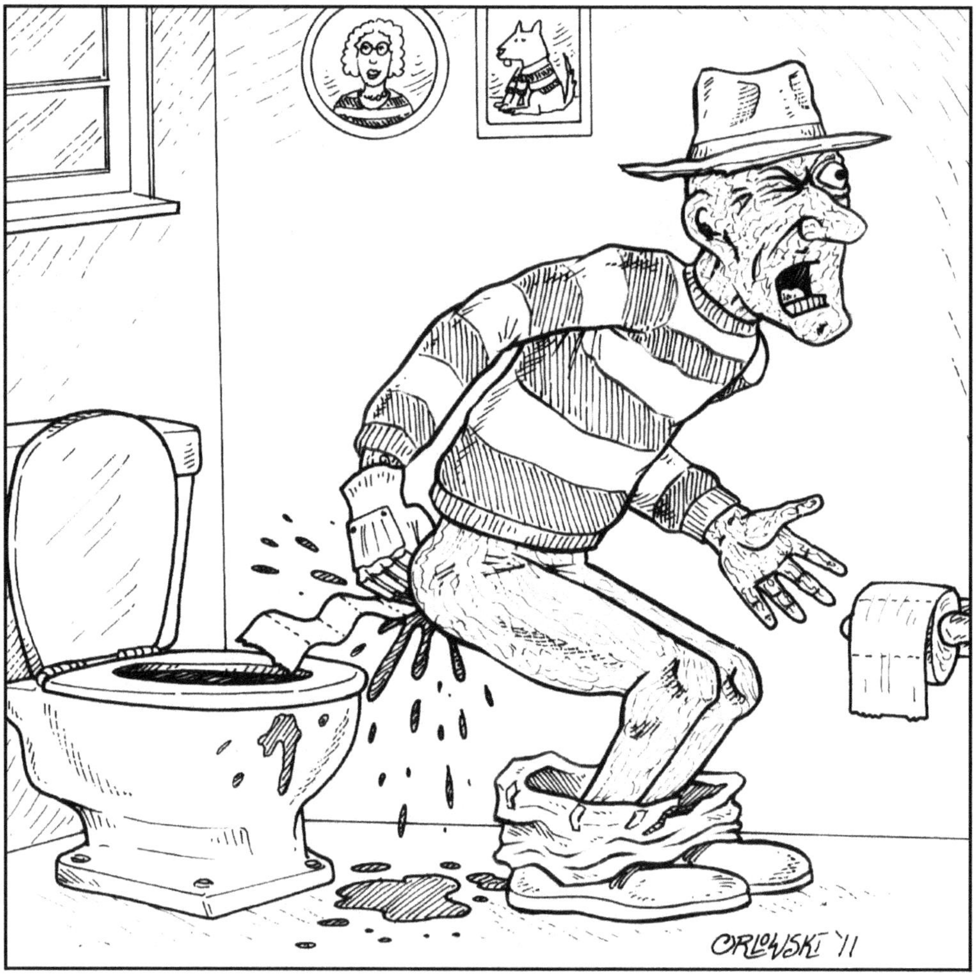
ORLOWSKI '11

In his thirty plus years as a supernatural serial killer, Freddy never once forgot to remove his bladed glove before wiping—and he would never, ever forget again.

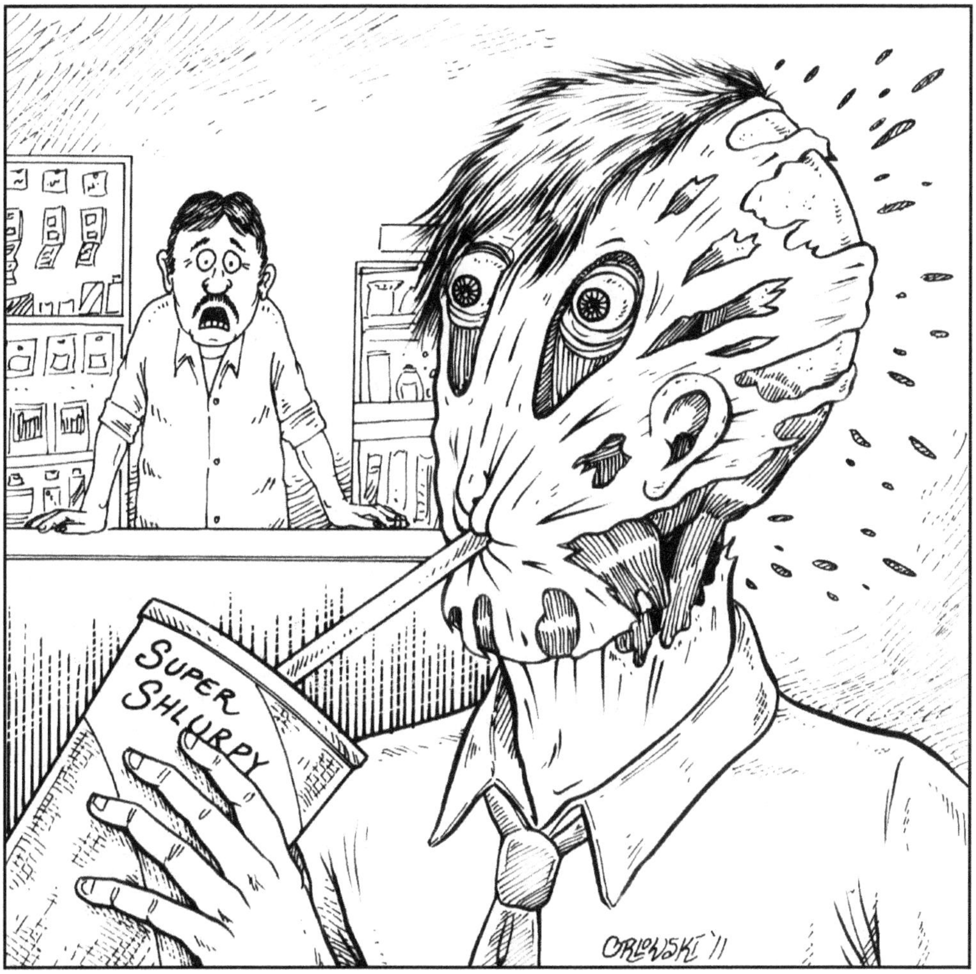
Super Shlurpy
ORLOWSKI '11

Richard only had a thirty-minute lunch and the Nifty-Mart was 14 minutes from his office, leaving him a two minute window to suck down the extra-thick Super Shlurpy.

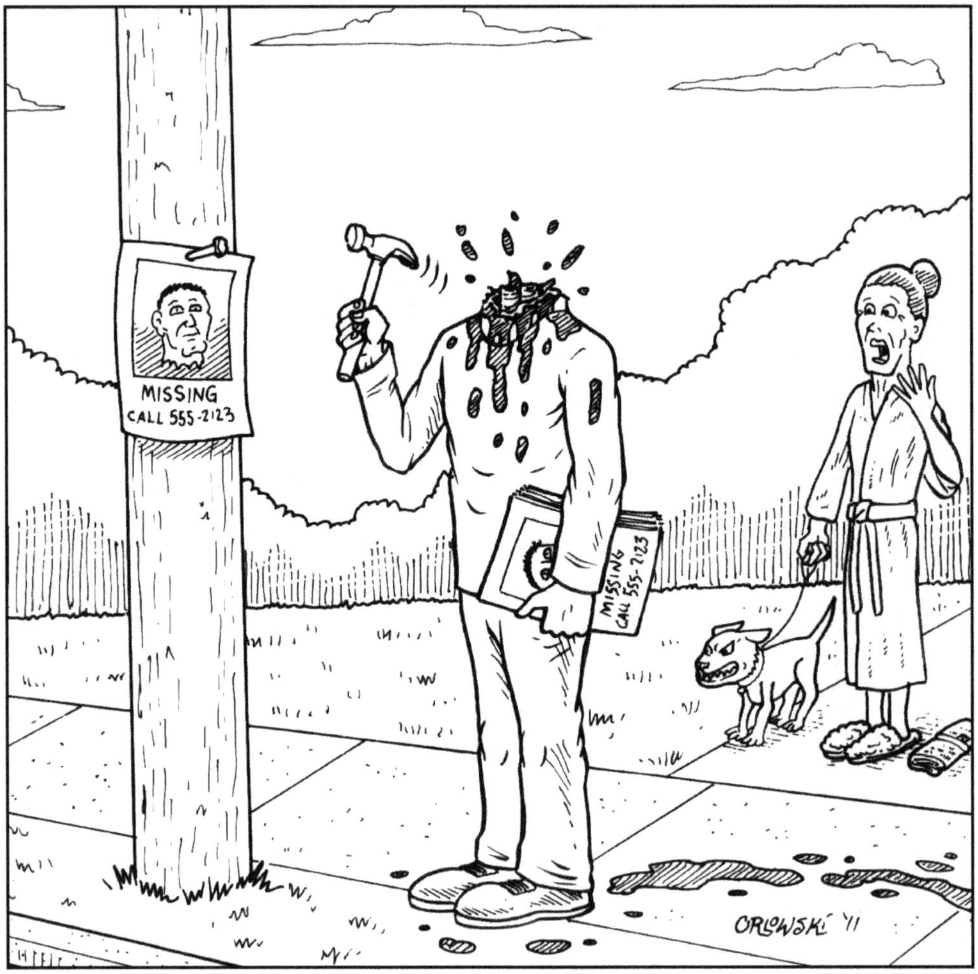
MISSING
CALL 555-2123
MISSING
CALL 555-2123
ORLOWSKI '11

Sal had once again lost
his head after a night out on the town
and, after placing posters advertising
his loss, he was unable to identify it
once it was found.

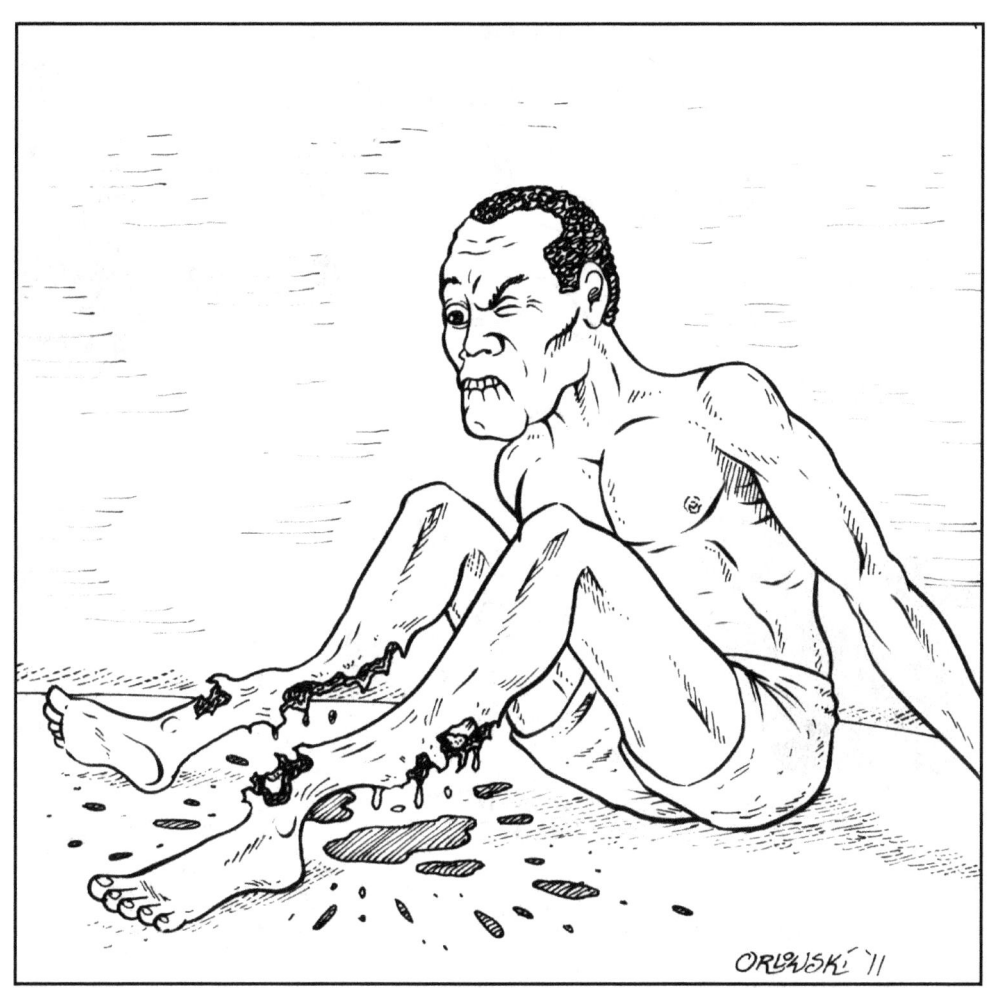

Andy's dream of being an
Olympic diver ended when he jumped into the pool
without looking first, but there were two positives:
first, he jumped feet first and second,
it was only the Special Olympics.

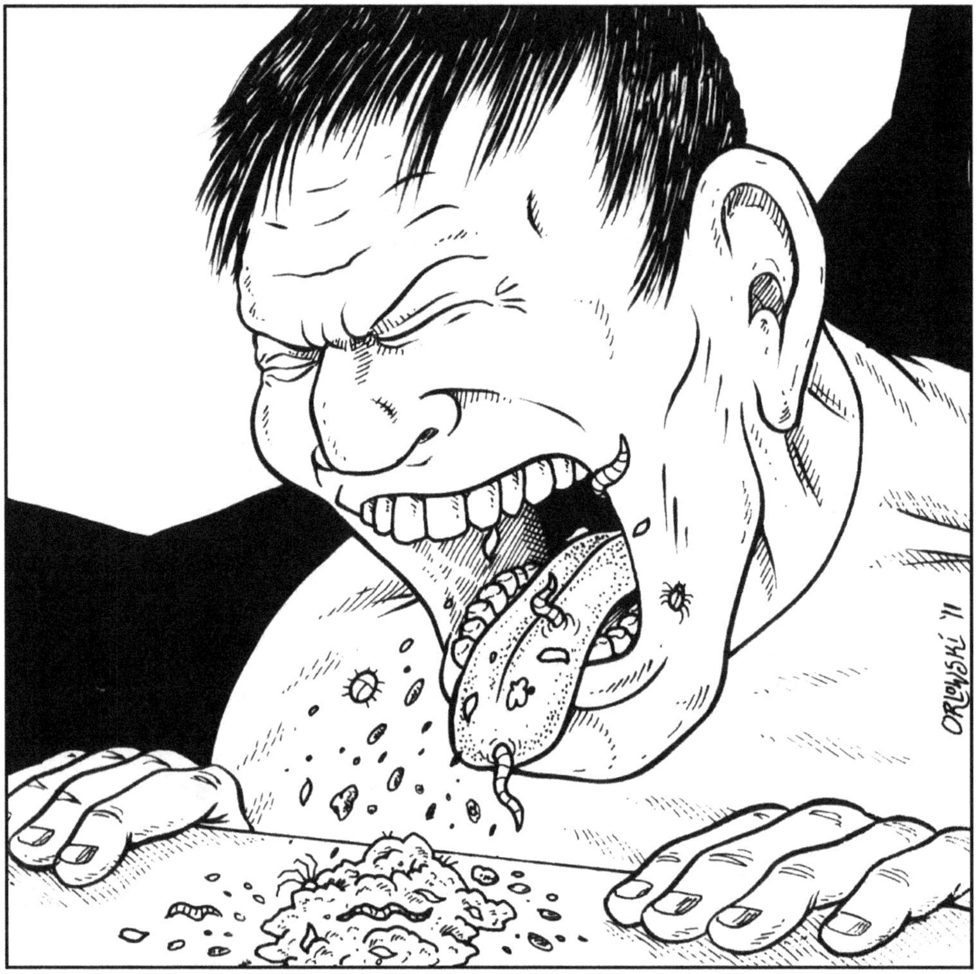
ORLOWSKI '11

Dominic coughed up a fetid wad
of wriggling worms, maggots, spiders and
beetles and finally went to the doctor's,
unable to shake this bug he caught.

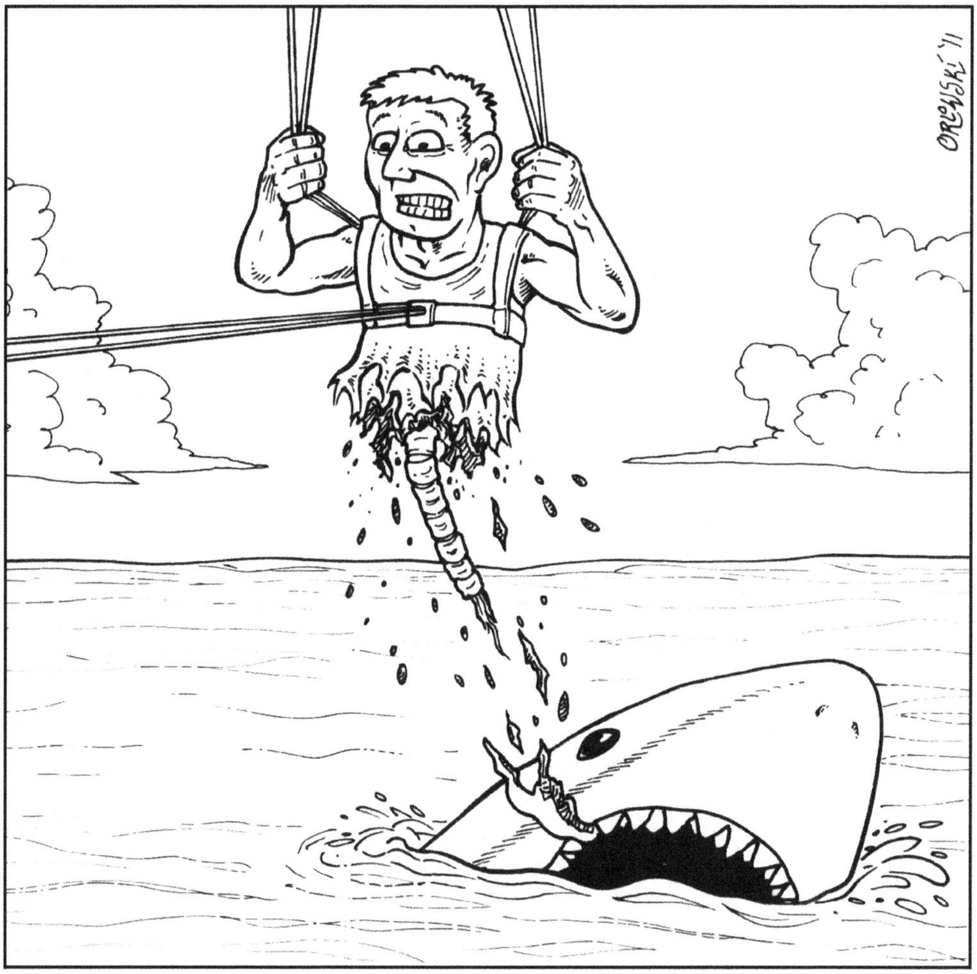
ORLOWSKI '11

Nolan was never a risk taker
but swore this vacation he'd try new things—
like the local emergency room.

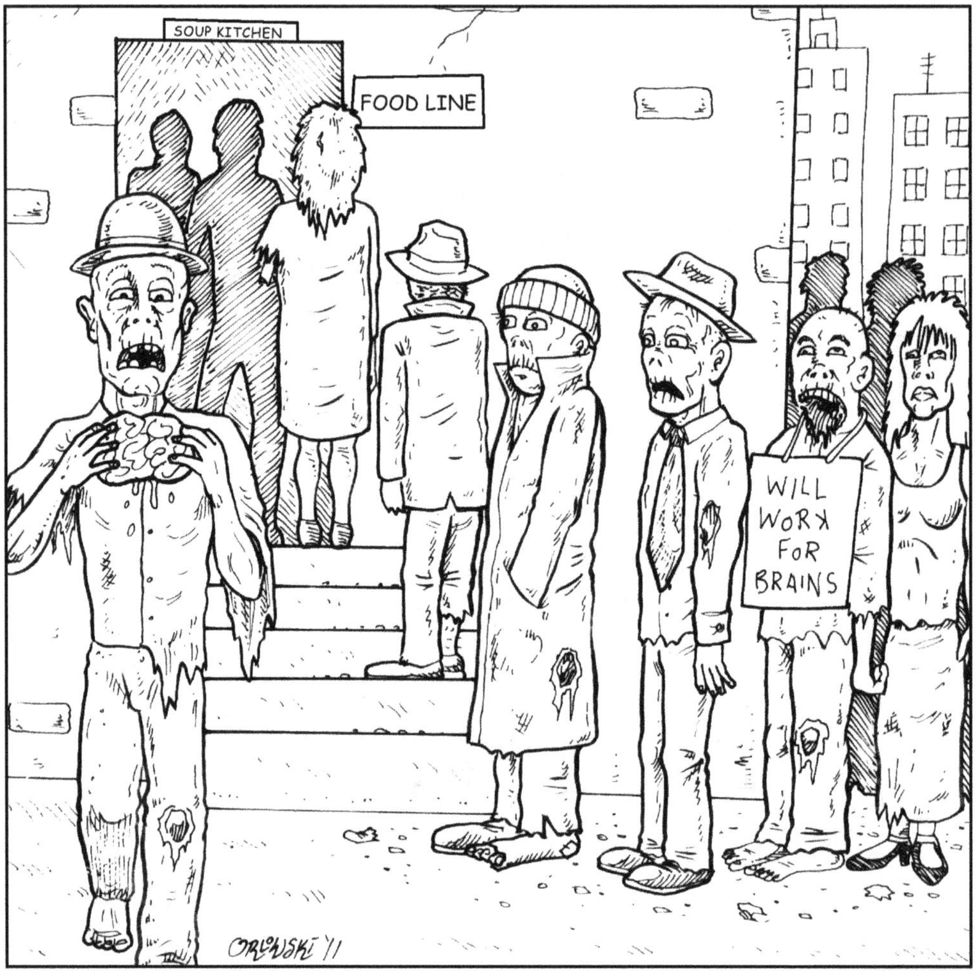
SOUP KITCHEN
FOOD LINE
WILL WORK FOR BRAINS
ORLOWSKI '11

Though the Great Depression was well documented in the lexicon of American History, little is included about the suffering of the undead.

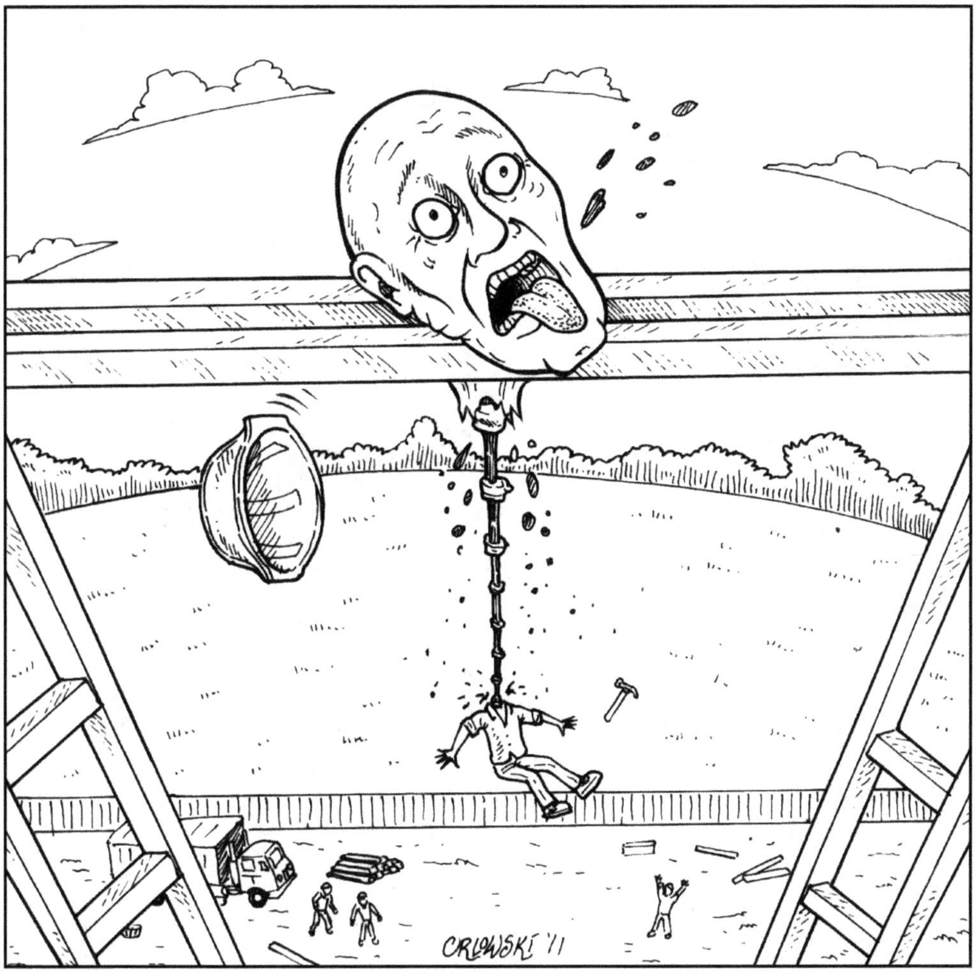
ORLOWSKI '11

'Fathead' Phil slipped through the girders and nearly fell to his death, but his big skull saved him, and though he learned to appreciate his old moniker, his friends started calling him 'Stretch'.

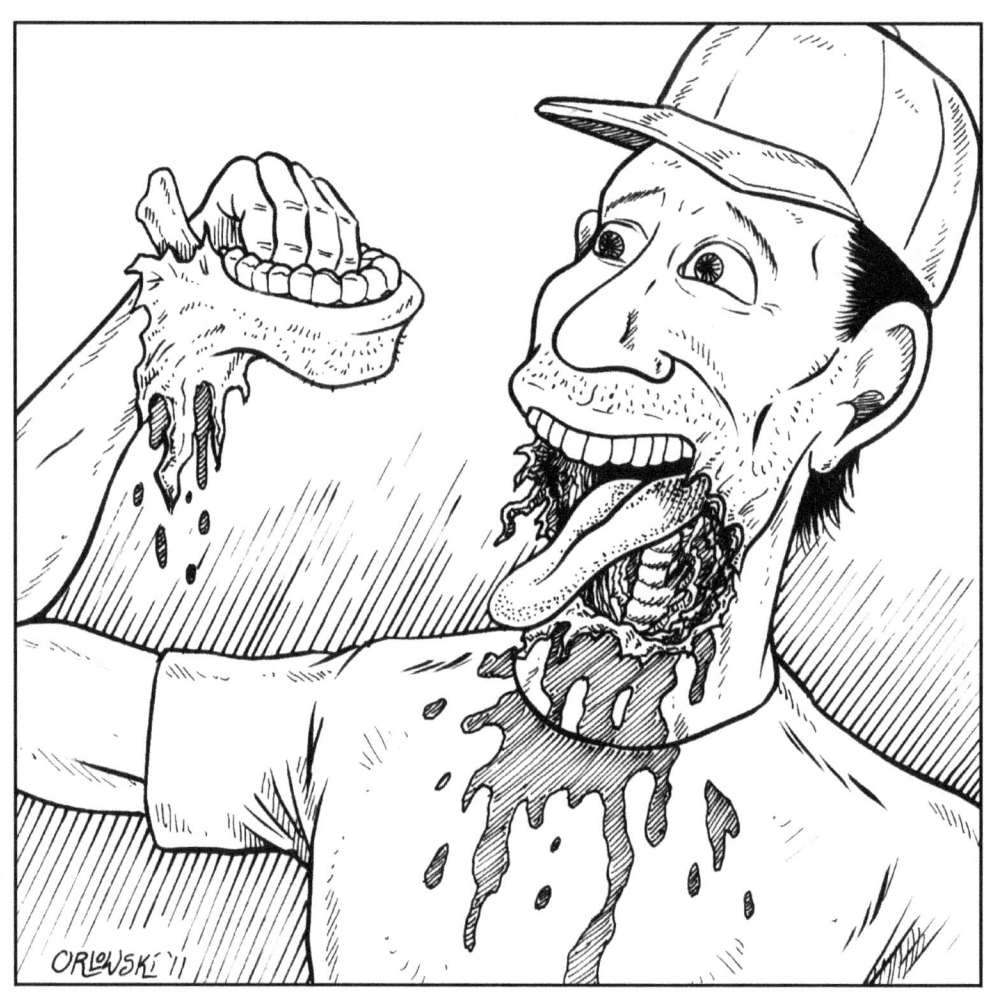
Jeb had always chewed tobacco thinking it was safer than smoking, and luck was on his side when his jaw became detached due to cancer and removed the tumors with it.

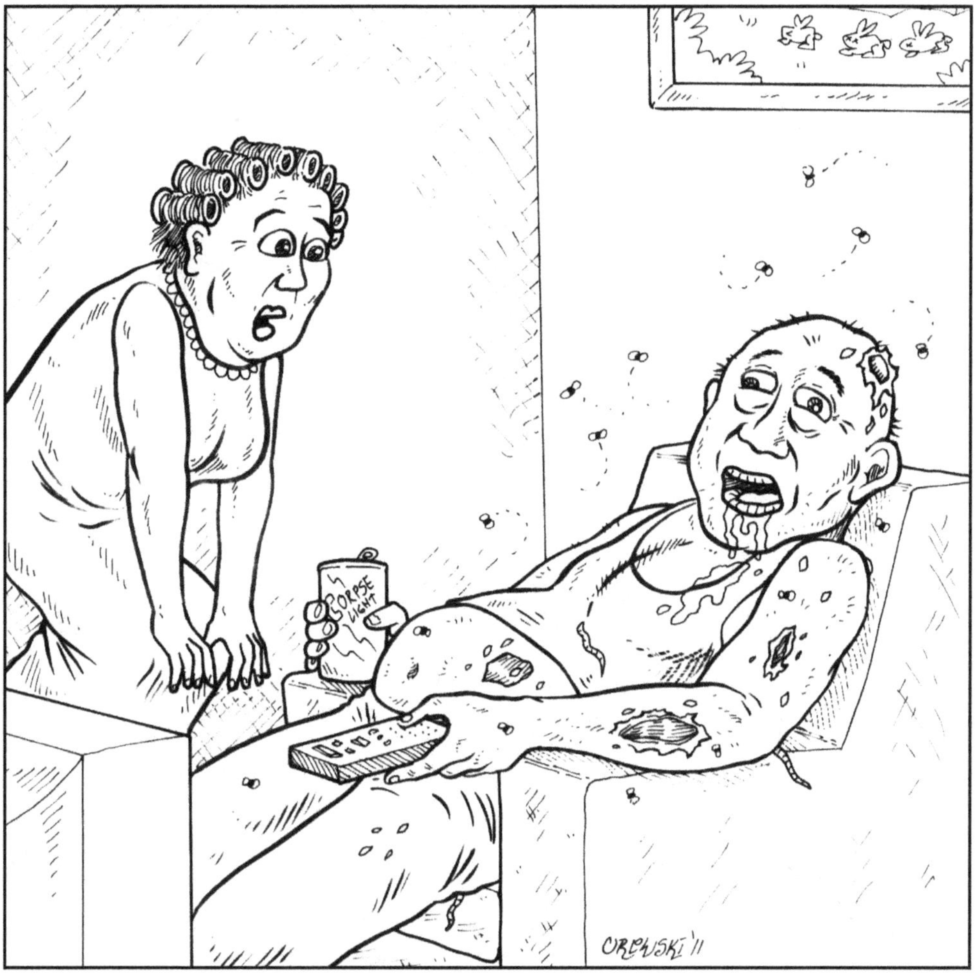
CORPSE LIGHT
ORLOWSKI '11

Martha felt it was normal that her husband wouldn't leave his chair for days, and the flies and foul odor were common, too, so she was shocked to learn he had been dead for several days.

Matt was an obstinate bastard and would go to great lengths to win an argument, even if it meant literally partaking in a dumb cliché.

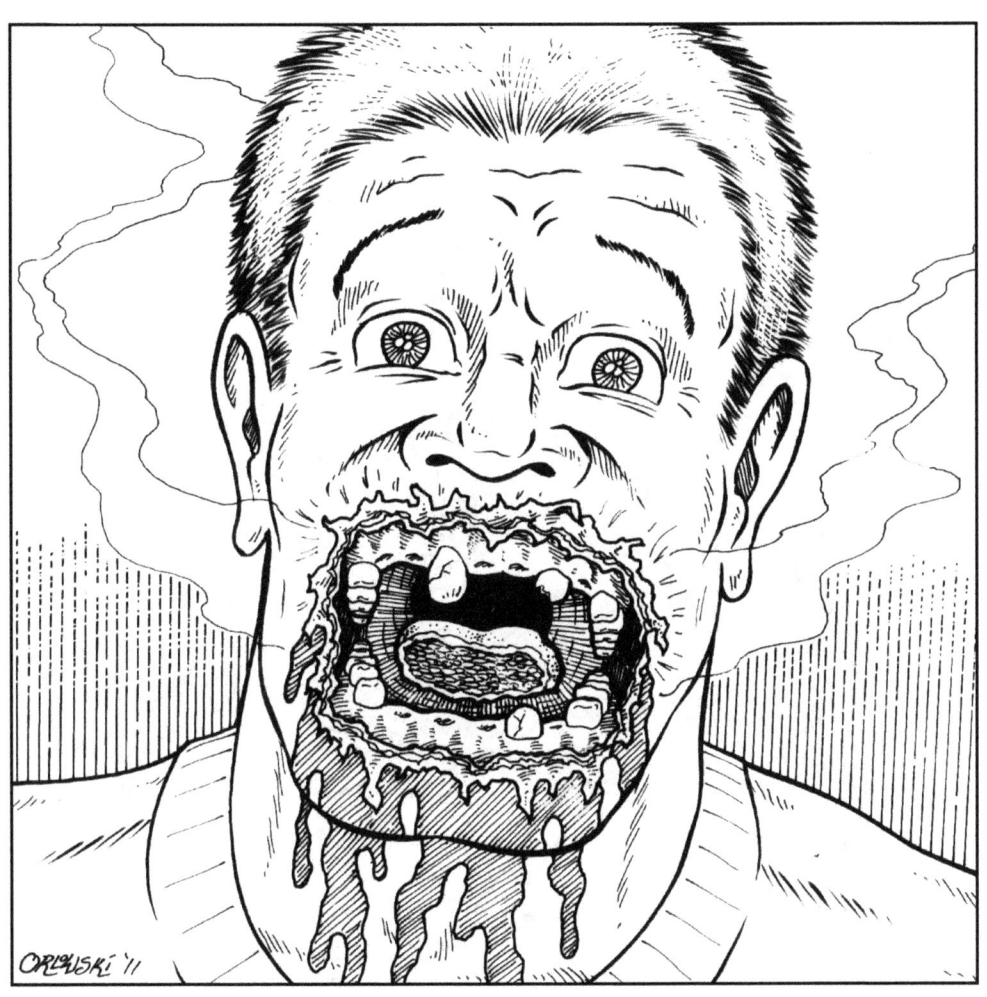

Smoking while drinking grain alcohol resulted in a horribly painful lesson and Mike ended up swearing off both bad habits, albeit non-verbally.

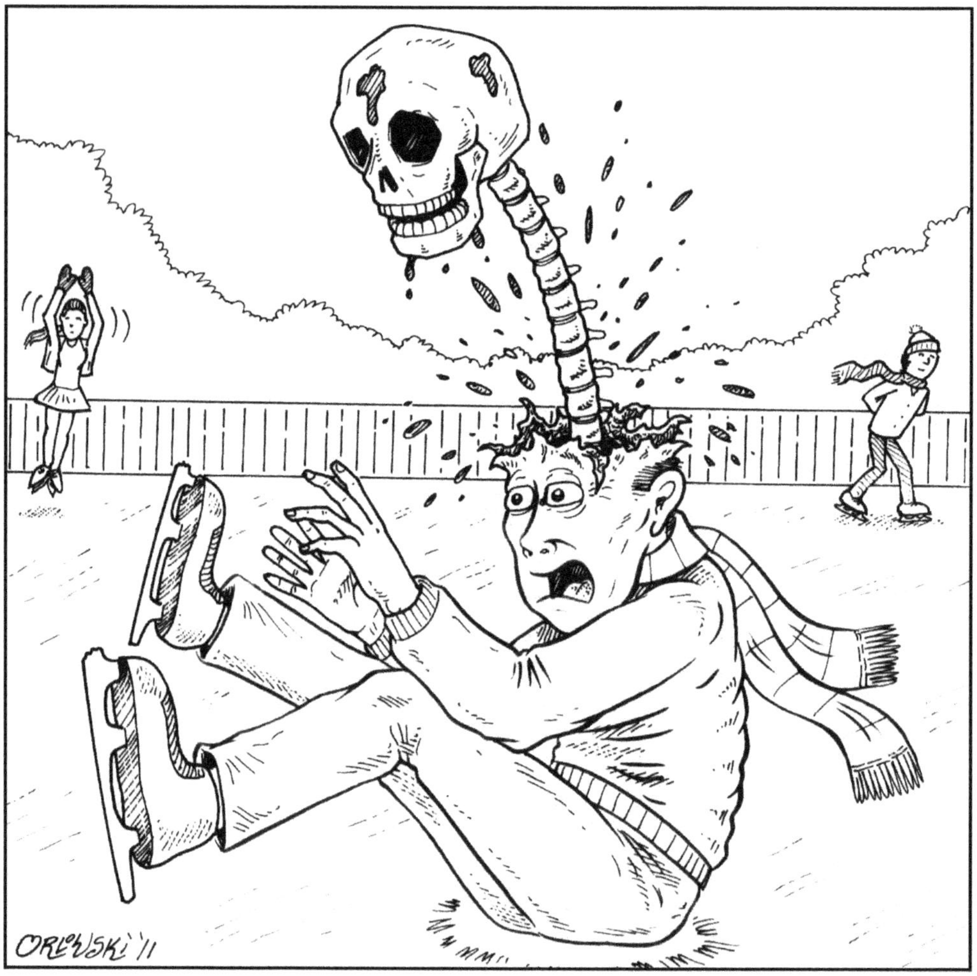
ORLOWSKI '11

Tim attempted the triple-axle but
failed and fell on his tailbone, propelling
his spine and skull upwards, ending his skating
career and starting his life as a vegetable.

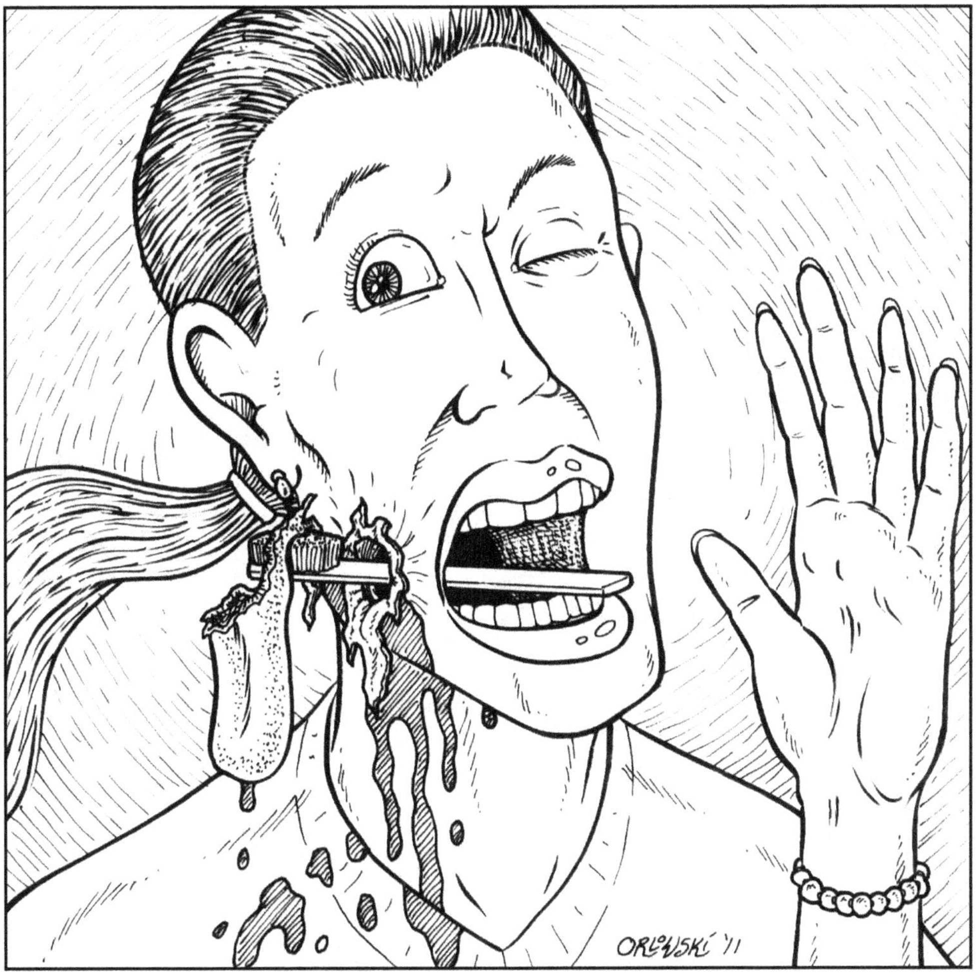
ORLOWSKI '11

Sarah was proud of her
pearly whites, so much so that she
brushed her teeth very hard, perhaps
a bit too fervently.

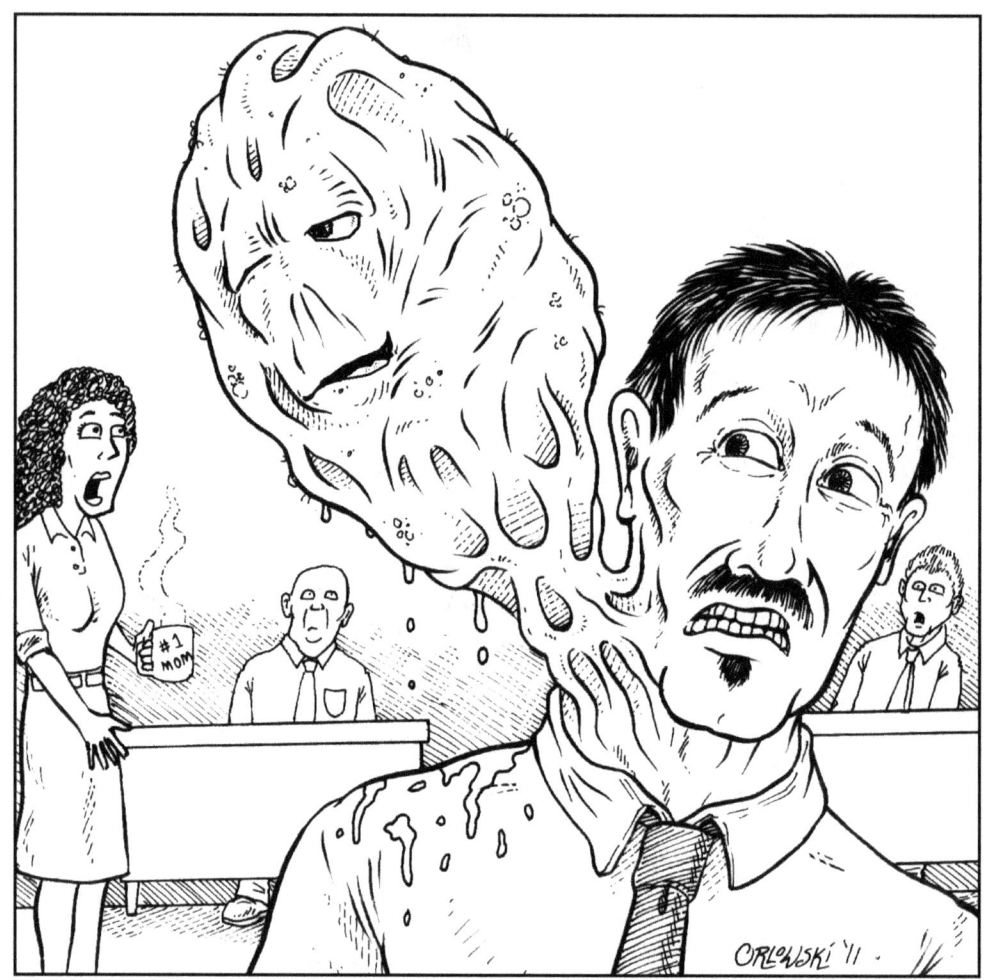

Fred wasn't too concerned with the growth on his neck, whether it be an awful tumor, alien pod or demon larvae, but that was before it started hitting on his female co-workers.

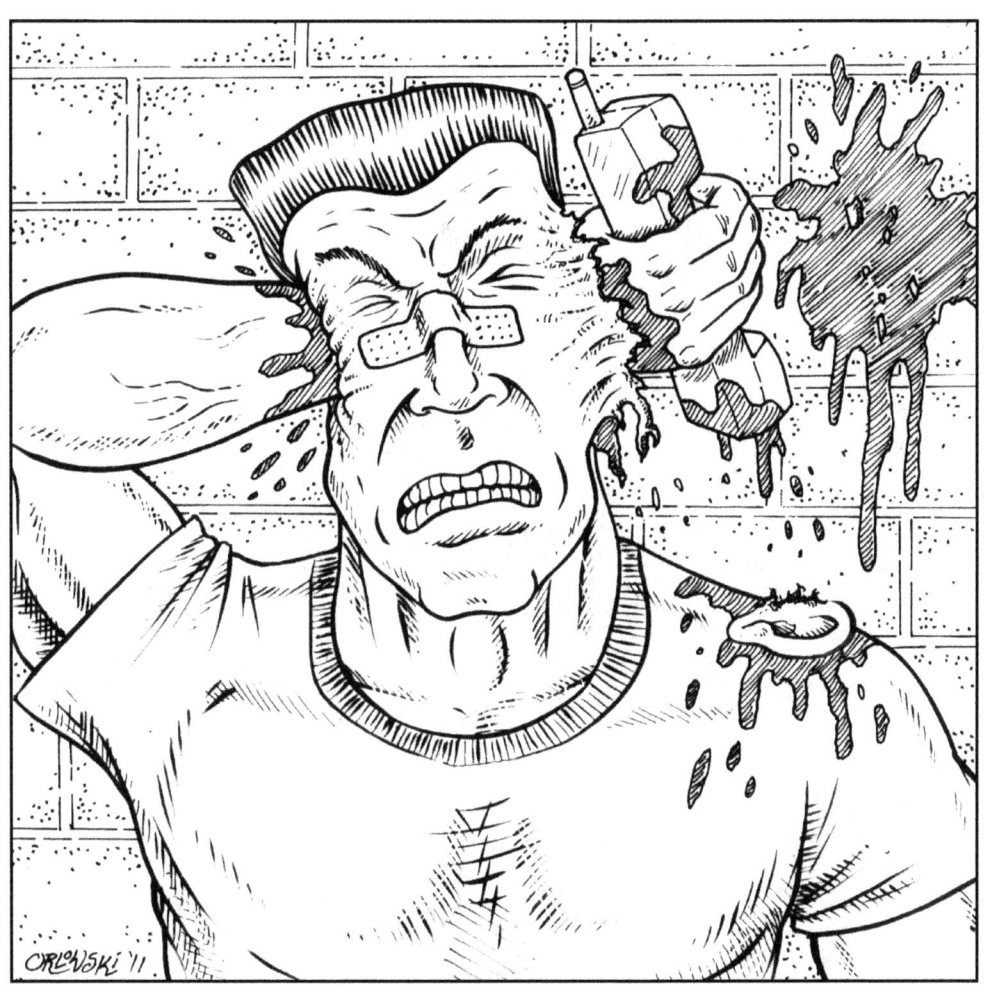
Superhuman George had finally healed
and had gotten Lasik so he wouldn't need glasses
anymore, but unfortunately rushed to answer the call
from the mayor on his superhero hotline.

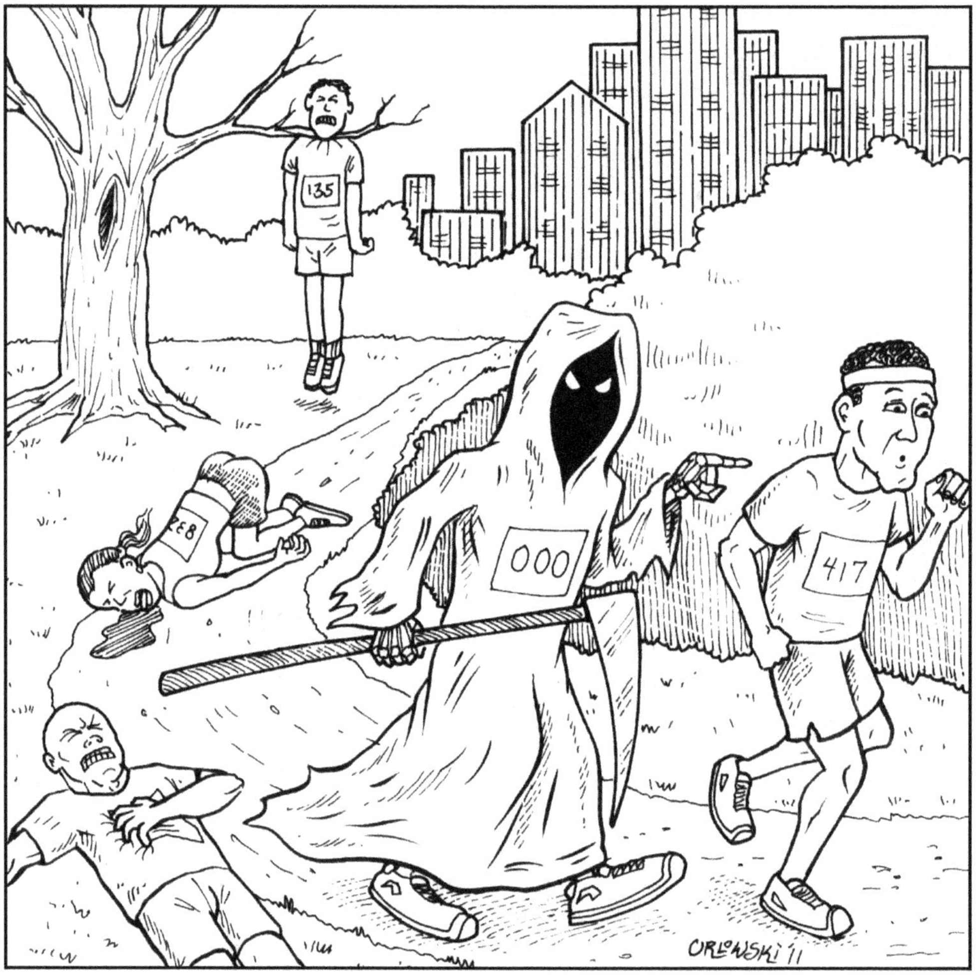
135
288
000
417
ORLOWSKI '11

Every year, Death dusted off
his sneakers and entered the marathon,
not just to dominate in the race, but to
decimate the competition.

Carol was upset, not only because she mistook the iron for the phone and melted half of her face, but she missed out on the call from a radio contest.

Sammy had never thought that while hanging around the pool flirting with the ladies that when someone yelled "Cannonball!" he'd actually be hit by one, but then again, he did live next to a Civil War Reenactment.

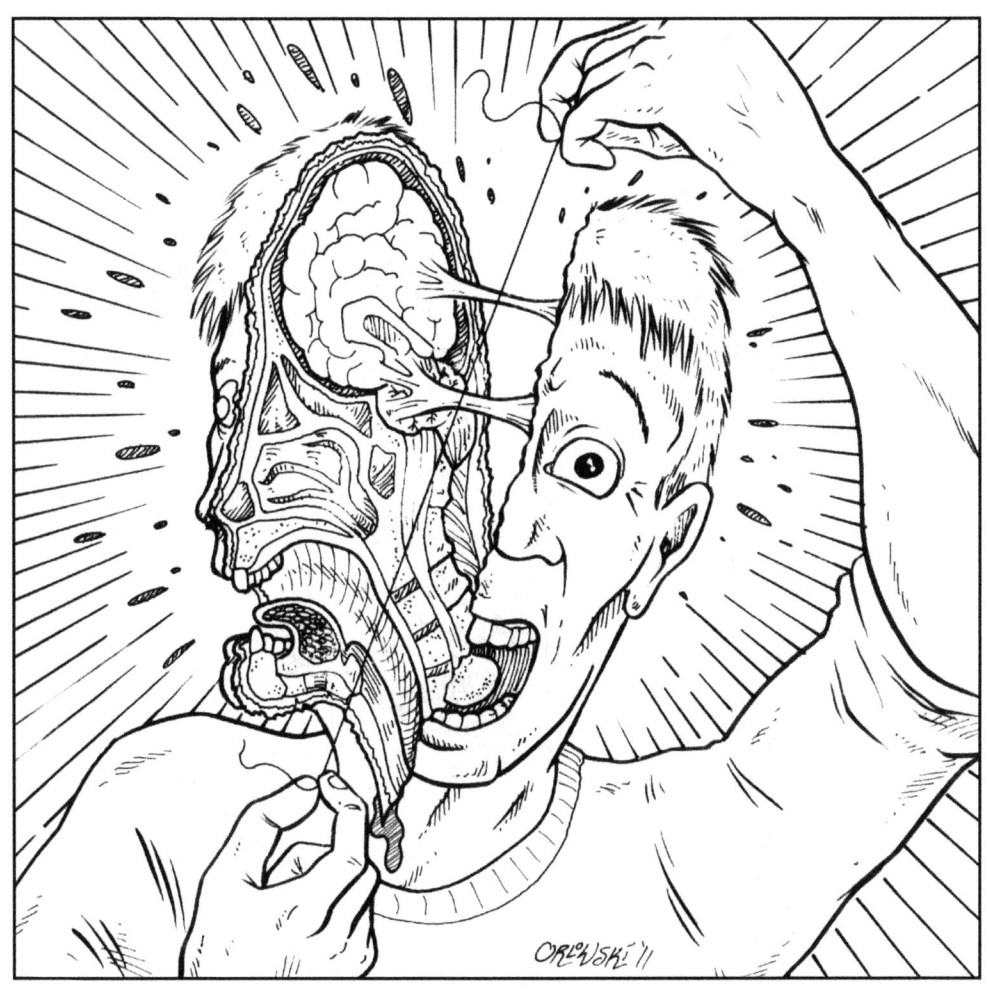

Skip ran out of dental floss and quickly used a guitar string, sadly that was moments before the earthquake hit.

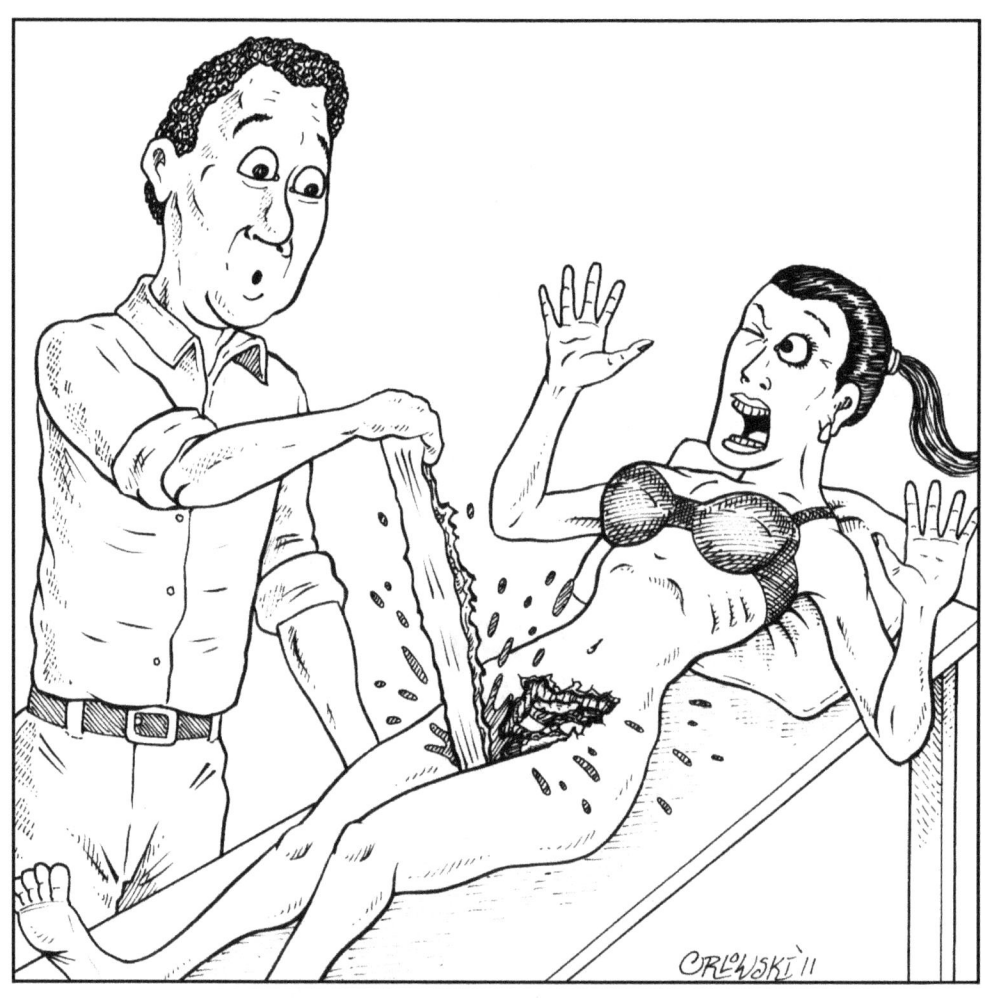

Neville instantly regretted
talking his wife into saving some money
and performing the Brazilian wax themselves
with some duct tape and glue.

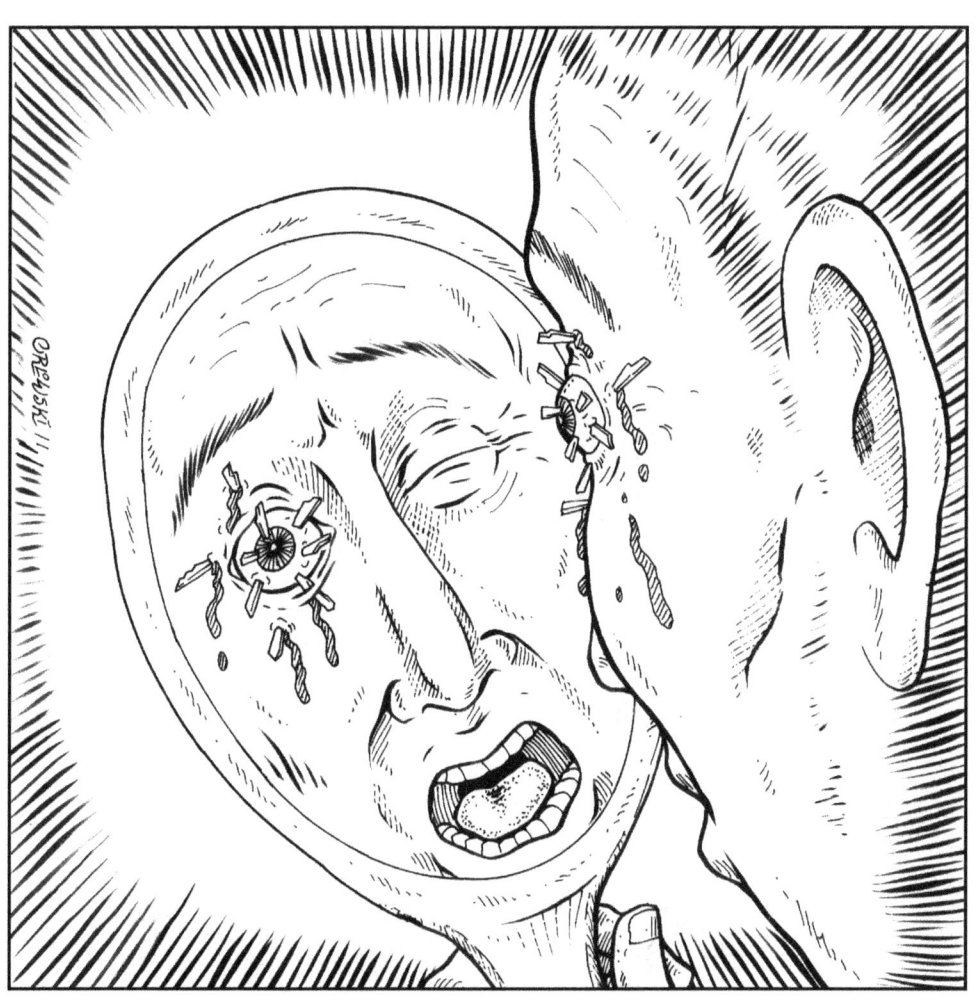

Harry finally learned
why it was a bad idea to keep his
contacts in the freezer.

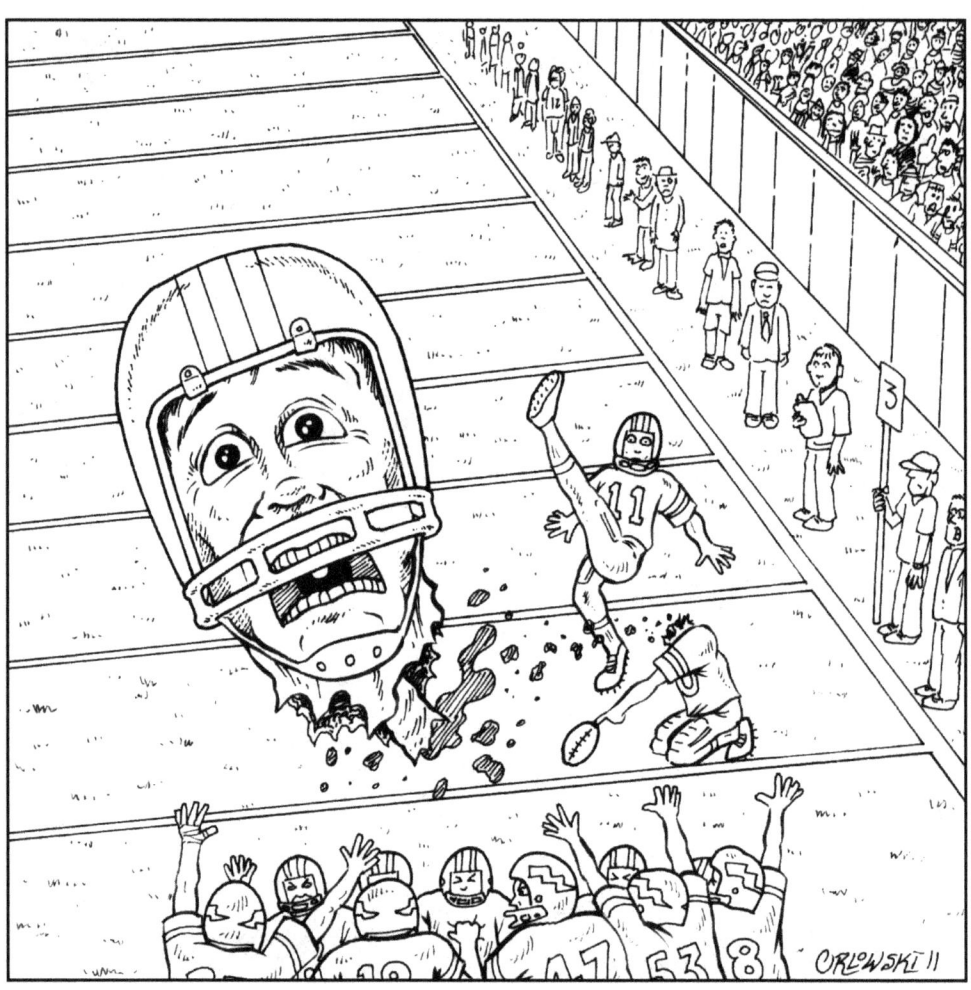

In his exuberance to clinch the win and be the hero, Zack kicked the placeholder's head through the uprights, and created the sports event forever known as 'Superbowl Bloody Sunday'.

WKPITU
BANDAGES
©RLEWSKI 11

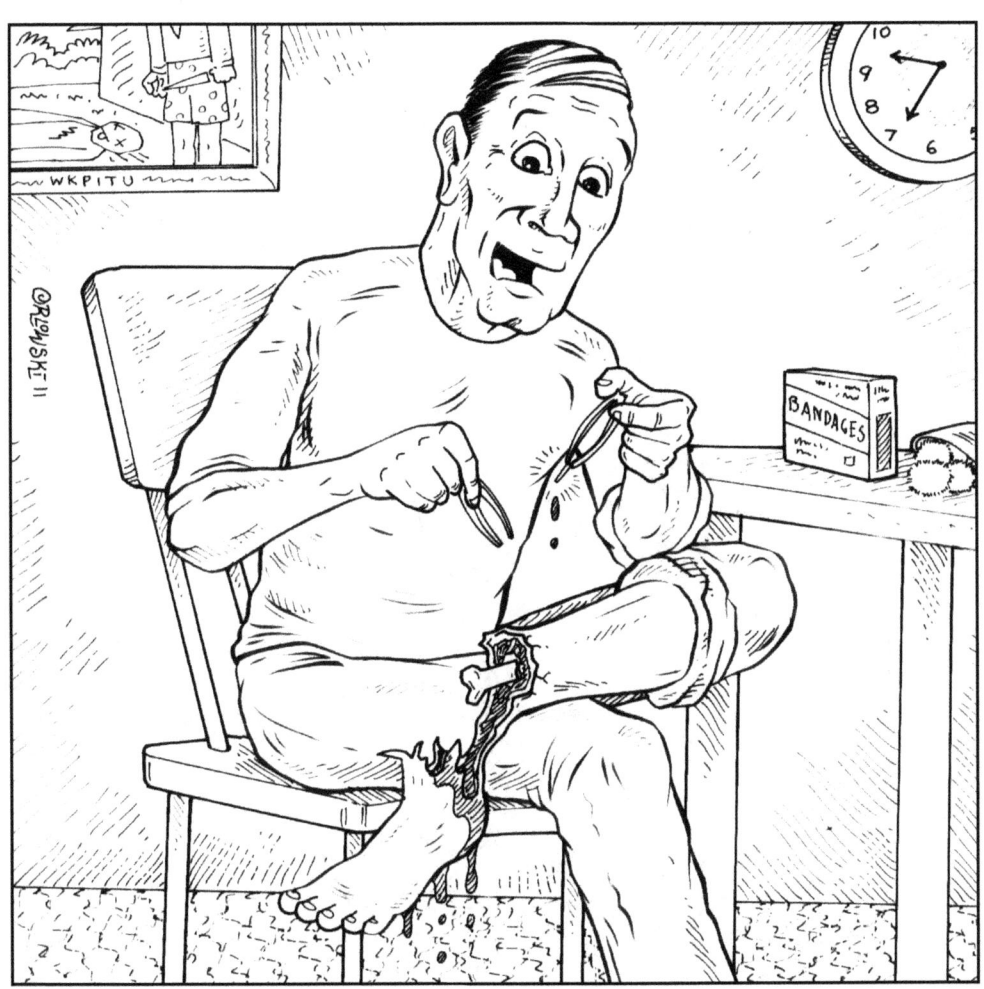

Wendel picked and picked
and finally pulled out the pesky splinter that
had made walking so uncomfortable.

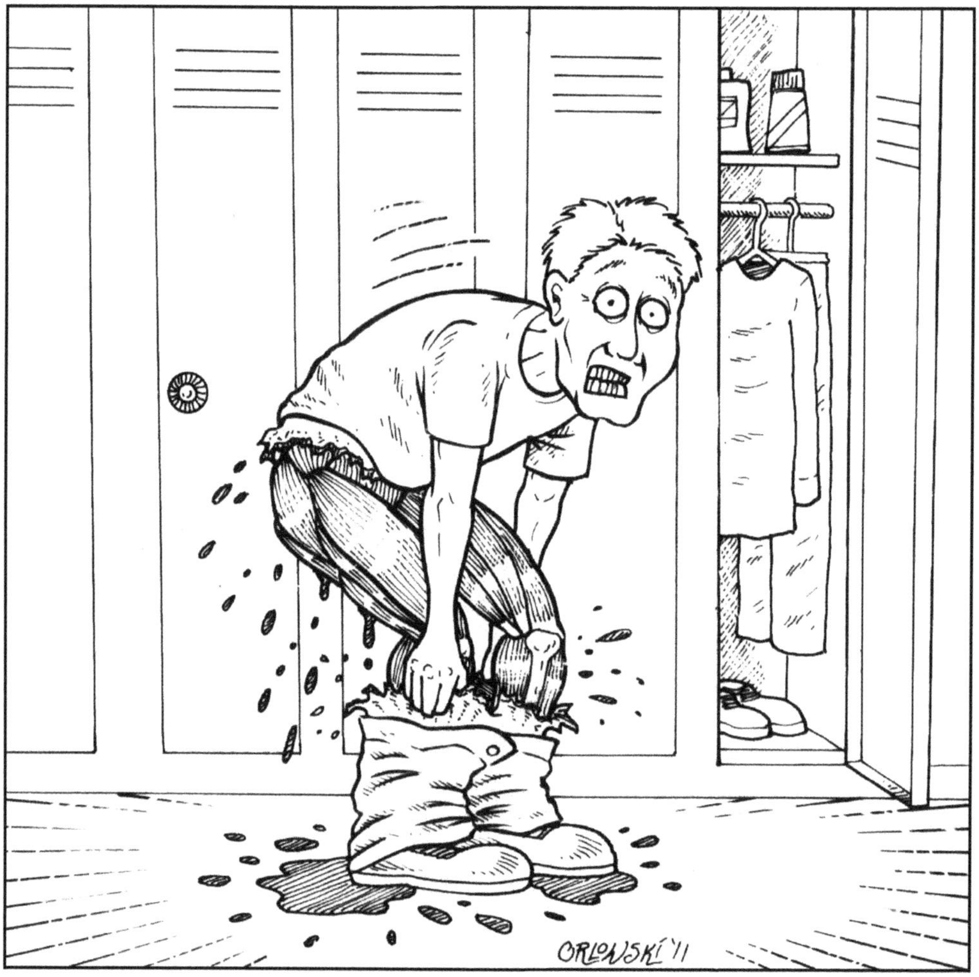
ORLOWSKI '11

Lenny, always the jokester,
wanted to quickly moon his buddies,
but in his rush, he accidently
grabbed his lovehandles.

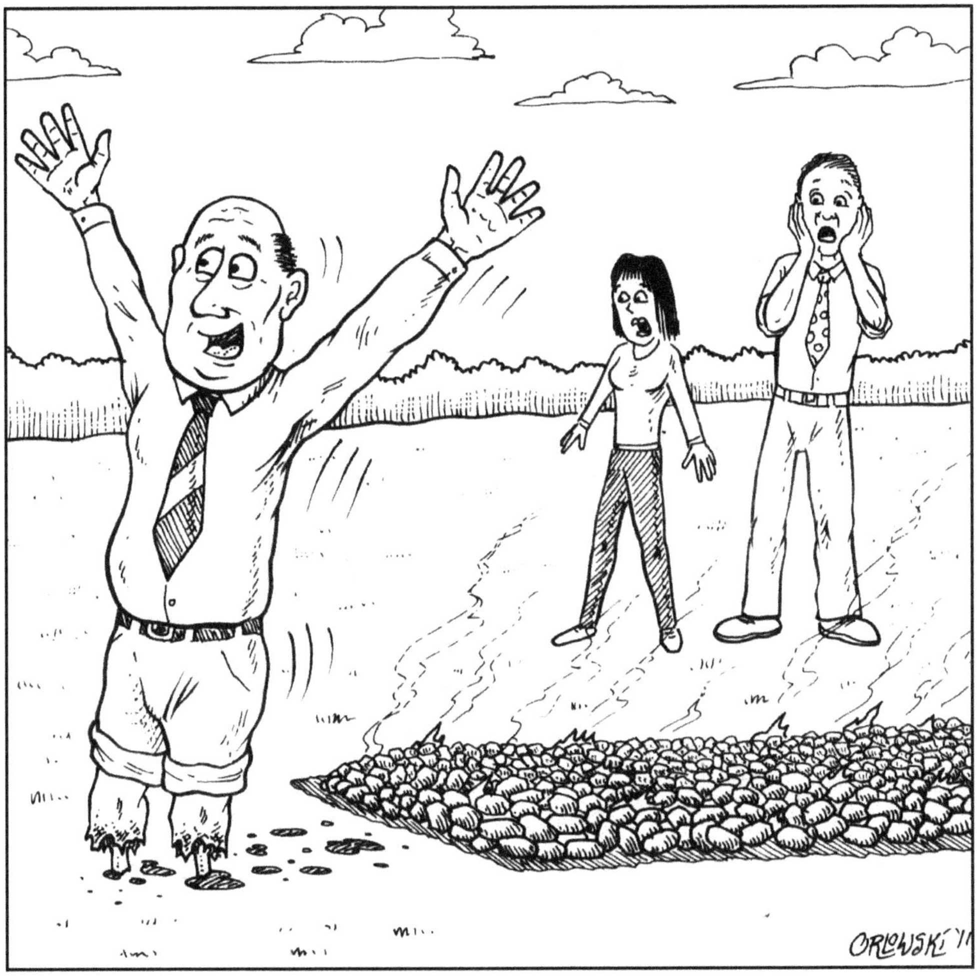
ORLOWSKI '11

Stu was proud to be the
first to cross the fire coals at the office
training exercise, and even happier that he no
longer had to work after the lawsuit.

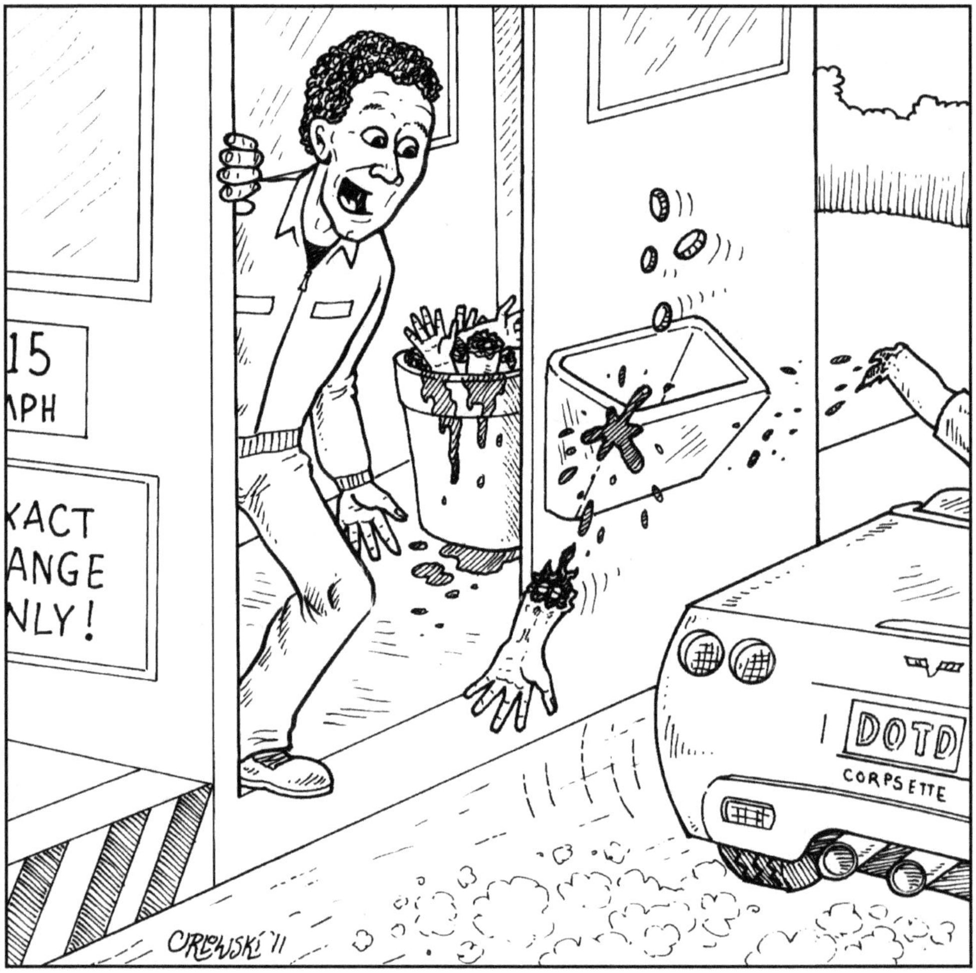
15
PH
XACT
ANGE
NLY!
DOTD
CORPSETTE
ORLOWSKI '11

Mortie had accumulated
quite the collection of severed hands
from commuters who refused to slow
down at the toll booth.

Oliver had no idea the MRI was on a timer, and when it kicked on he was reminded exactly how much metal was on and in his body.

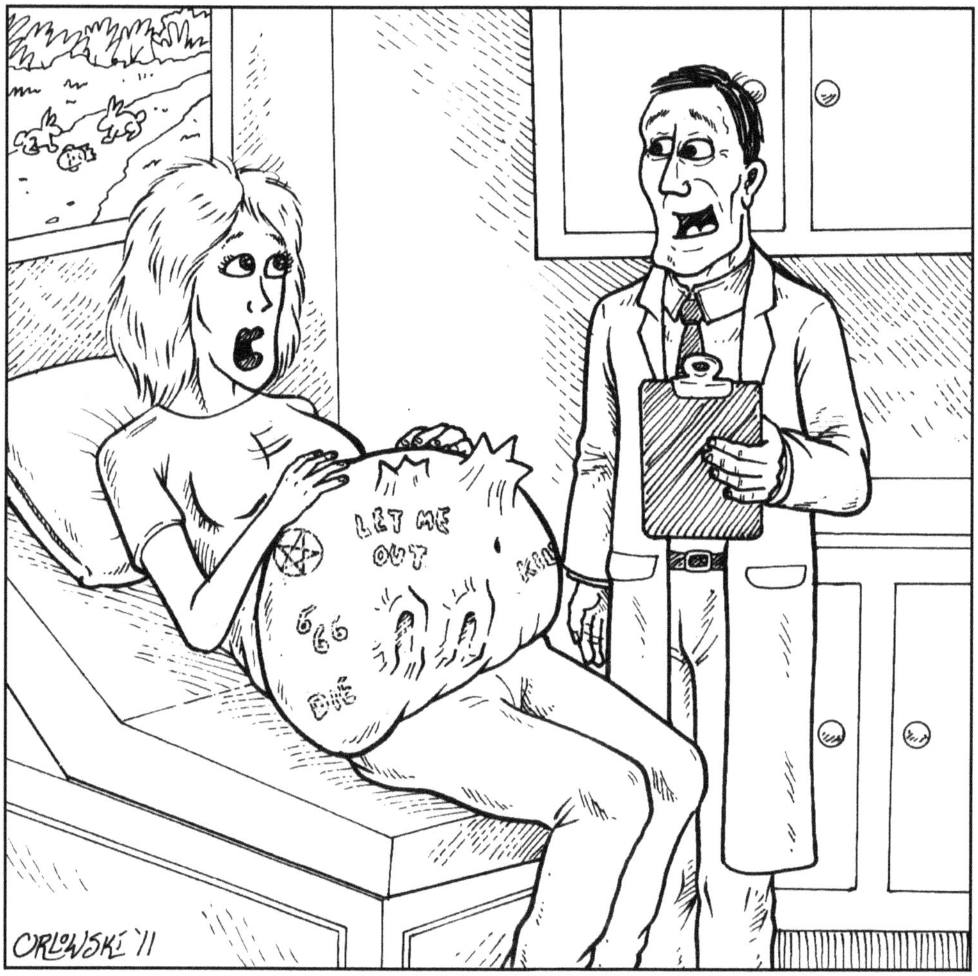
LET ME
OUT
666
DIE
ORLOWSKI '11

"Congratulations Miss Vicks,
you are giving birth to a happy, healthy,
and fiendishly diabolical Antichrist."

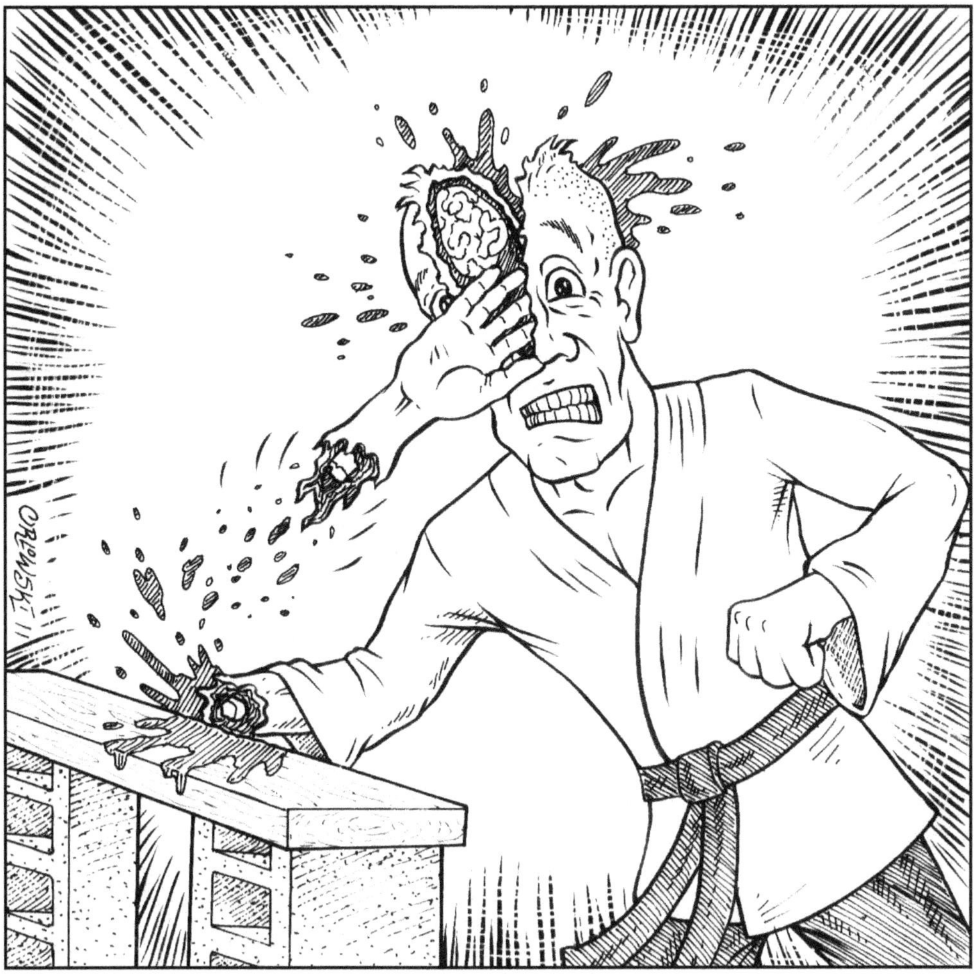
ORLOWSKI

Jay knew he blew the demonstration when his own hand split his face, but he still managed to impress his sensei and earn his black belt.

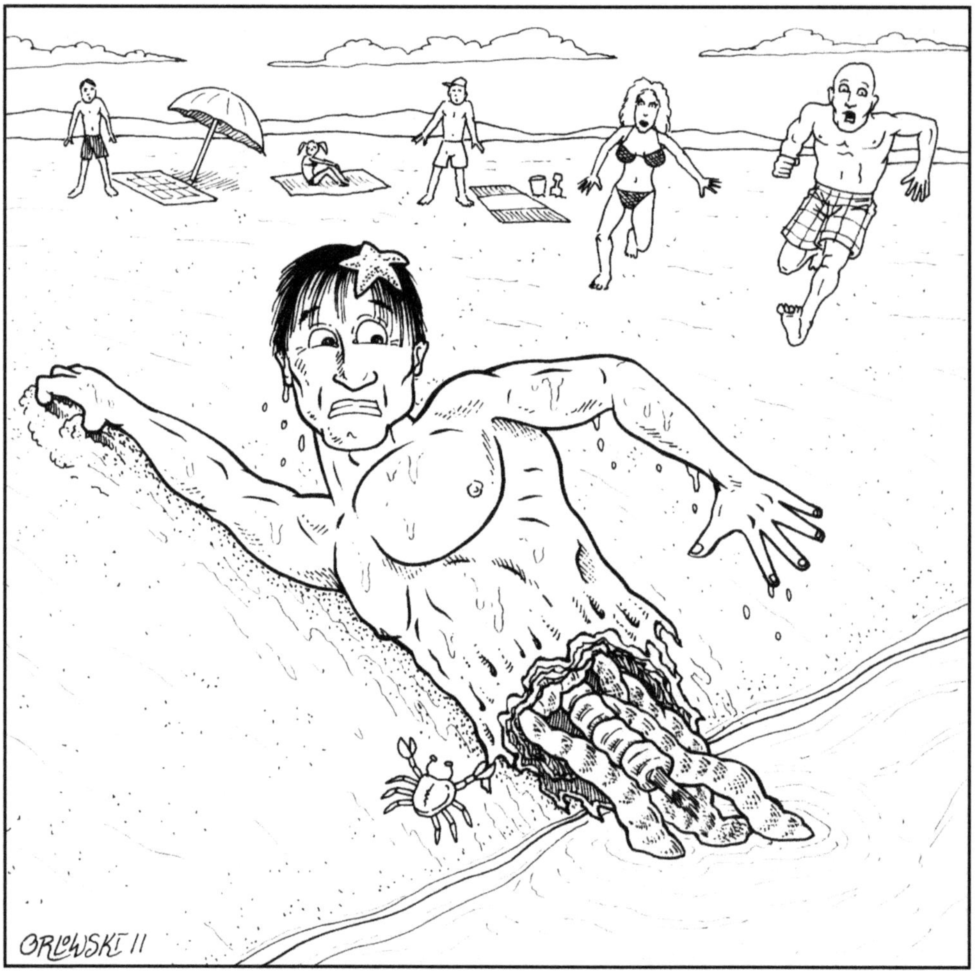
ORLOWSKI 11

Kevin survived a severe shark attack and swam against riptides to save himself, it was no surprise the newspapers declared him The Buoy Wonder.

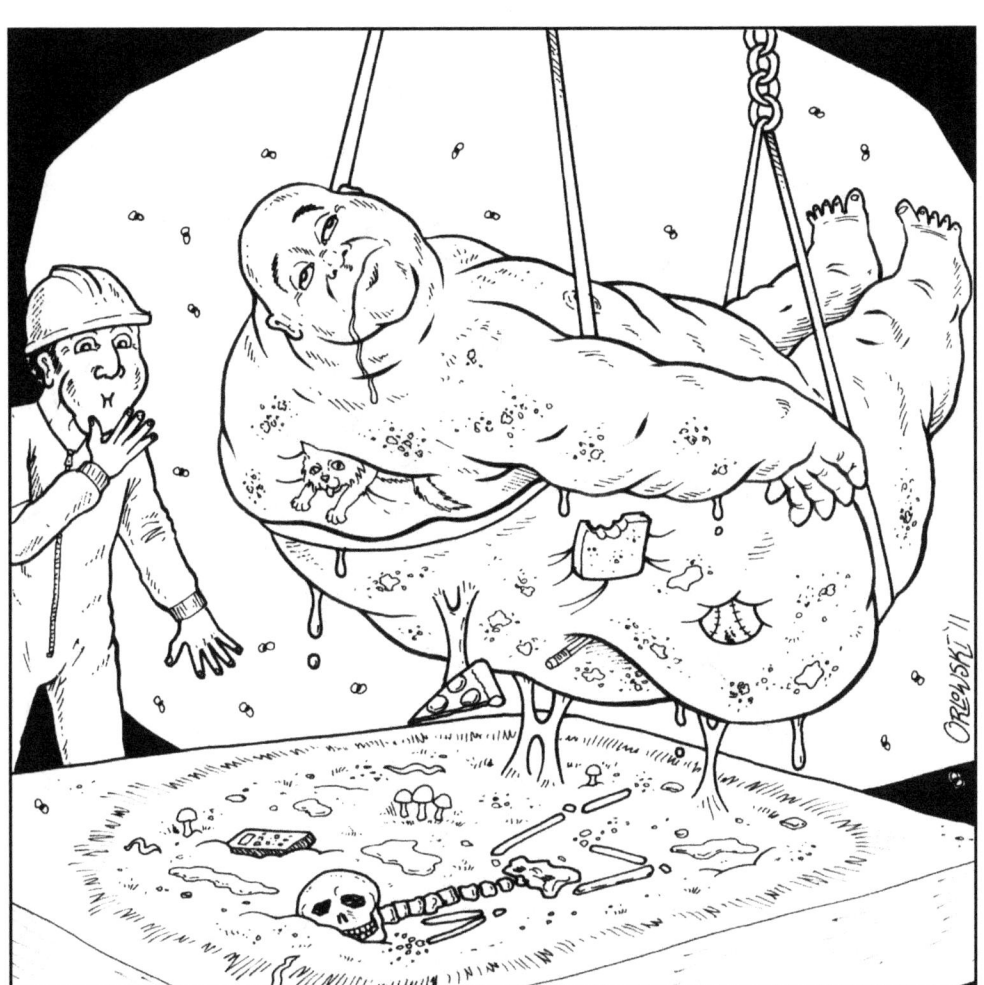

When Big Al was finally winched from his deathbed, the removal crew found plenty of rotten food, a No. 2 pencil, a remote, a baseball signed by Thurman Munson, the skeleton of Aunt Edna, and the remains of Mr. Fuzzies, Al's cat who'd gone missing weeks before.

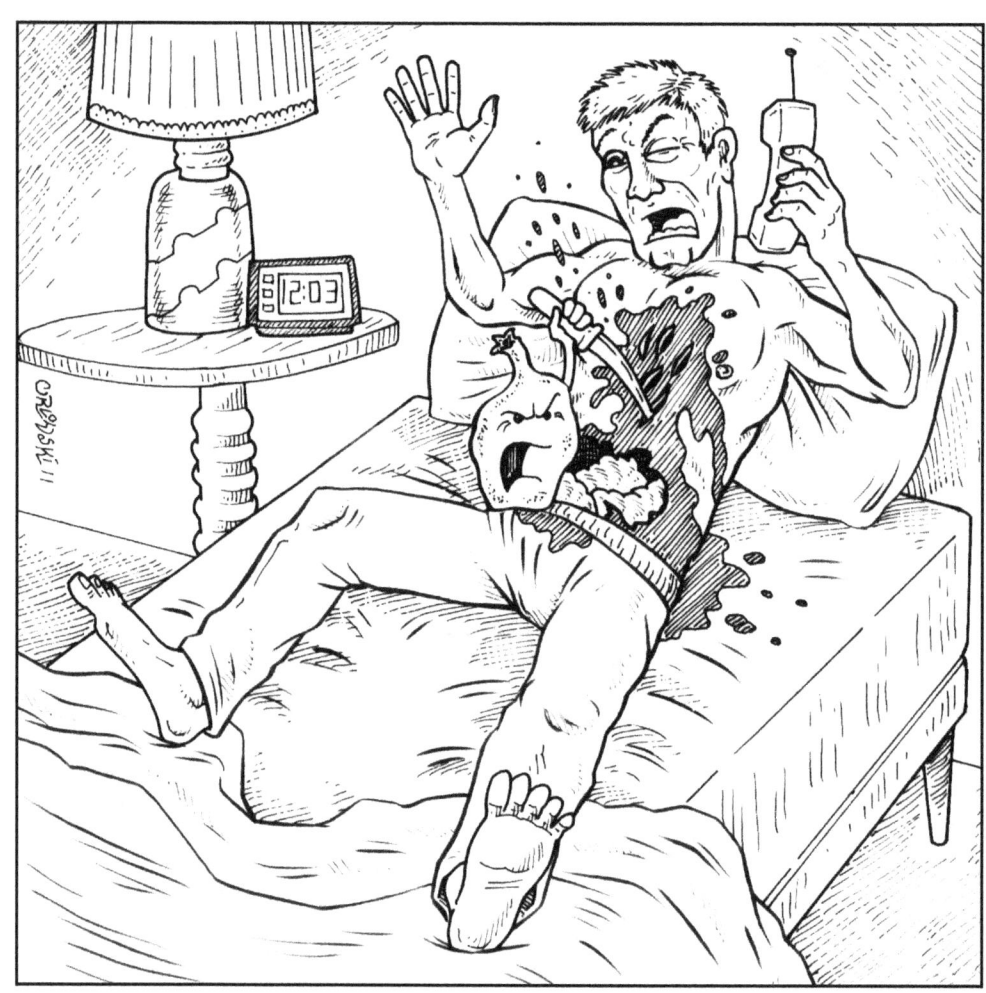

Harvey couldn't really blame the 9-1-1 dispatcher for hanging up on him when he called in that his stomach was killing him.

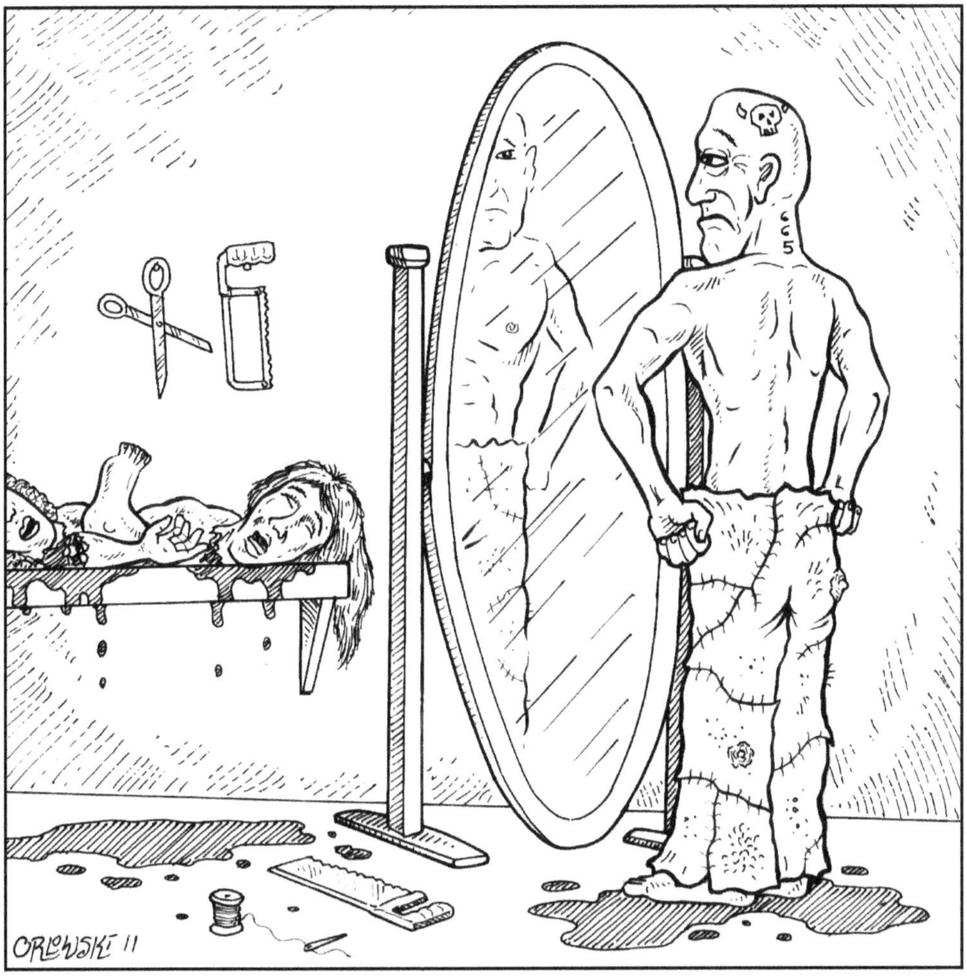
ORLOWSKI '11

After months of killing
and skinning his victims, Psycho Bob
was left wondering if his human-skin
pants made him look fat.

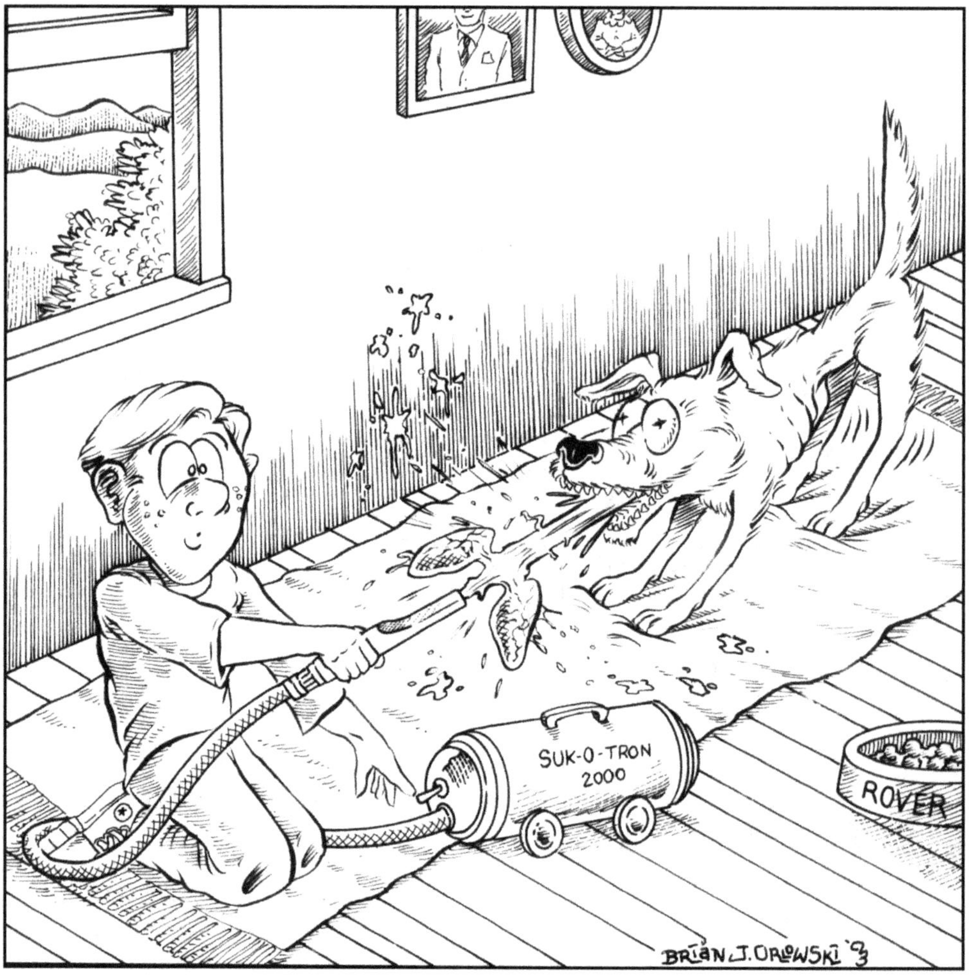
SUK-O-TRON
2000
ROVER
BRIAN J. ORLOWSKI '93

Jimmy sucked out Rover's lungs, instantly killing his best buddy, and wondered if the furnace was the best method of disposal.

Author's Note: This was actually one of the very first Strange Guts created. I initially removed it from all submissions because it suggested cruelty towards animals. I included it in this compendium purely to complete the history of the cartoon series. I am a fan of animals, would never hurt an animal, and in no way promote cruelty towards them. I have a wonderful dog and an antisocial cat and I adore them both.

Please donate your time or money to your nearest no-kill shelter.

Caption Contest Winner
Kain McGhee, Tennessee

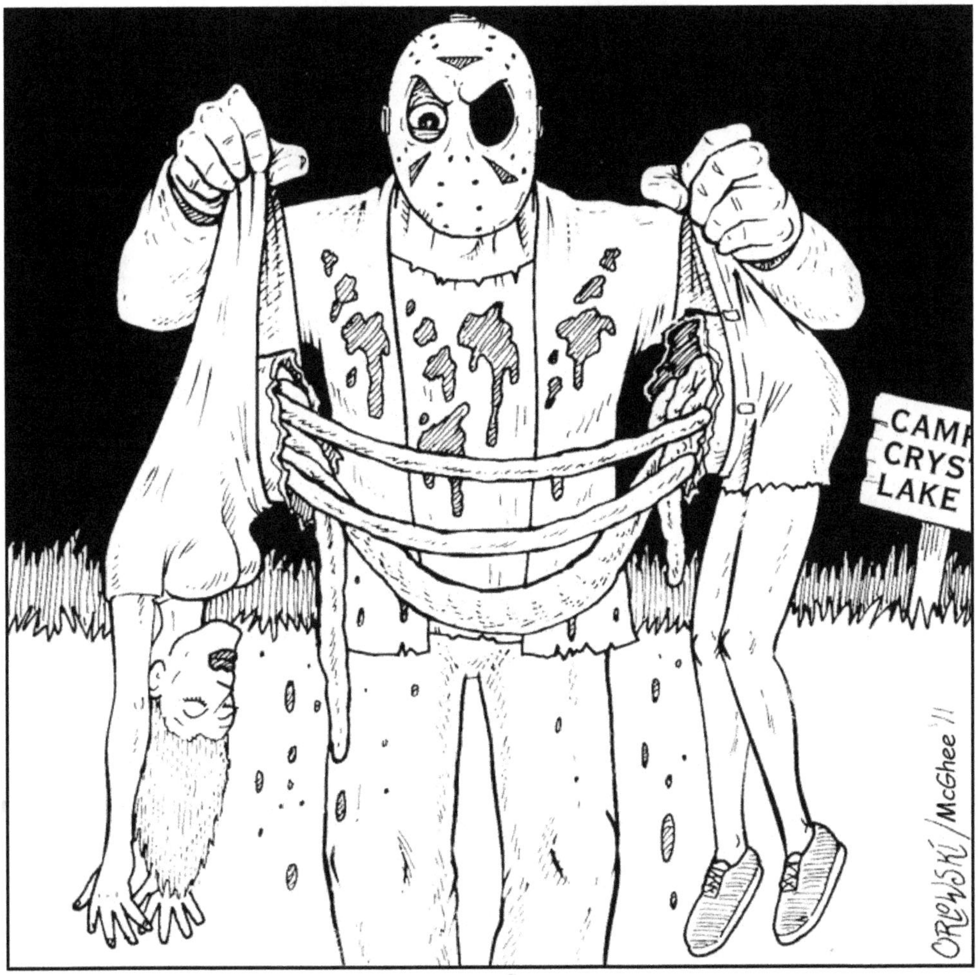
CAMP
CRYST
LAKE
ORLOWSKI/McGhee '11

Picnic with Jason—
leg and thigh or
wing and breast?

www.ingramcontent.com/pod-product-compliance
Lightning Source LLC
Chambersburg PA
CBHW081332090426
42737CB00017B/3112